Contact Information

Mule and Muse Productions, LLC
2892 Alcoa Hwy
Knoxville, TN 37920
Fax = 865 579-2522
Web Site: muleandmuseproductions.com
Email: info@muleandmuseproductions.com

Direct tax deductable contributions can be made to
The Greater Living Institute (GLI)
at 2892 Alcoa Hwy, Knoxville TN 37920

CPSIA information can be obtained at www.ICGtesting.com
Printed in the USA
LVOW020416130513

333459LV00001B/1/P

I Might Be You: An Exploration of Autism and Connection

by

Barb Rentenbach
and
Lois Prislovsky, Ph.D.

ISBN: 978-0-988-34490-7
Library of Congress Control Number 2012949628

About the Book

Did you hear the severe autism alert sirens wailing? Did that storm luckily miss you and yours? Not us. Our family took a direct hit. I Might Be...You is a fresh look at the damage and emerging sun, as told by an adult with autism who is "disguised as a poor" but, has much to say, yet does not speak and a therapist who helps rebuild. With experience, wit, warmth, and wisdom, these two collaborate to rethink roles, expectations, treatment strategies, education, meaning, and the healing truth about connection. It is a must read for overwhelmed parents, teachers, and practitioners needing inspiration, and those with ASD seeking purpose as hope is found.

As you enjoy this highly entertaining, thought-provoking, and deeply emotional account of life with autism, we invite you to discover who you might be and the unique contributions that may be yours to make.

After all, "without you, I would not be me." (Native American Proverb)

Preface

This book is presented in two parts. The first is reflection products from the first five years we worked together. The second section is current thoughts about who we are now after connecting with each other and what we learned about autism and related topics. We wish you all a refreshing read filled with childlike joy and wisdom.

Sincerely,
Barb and Lois

Note from Barb on how this book was written:

Our style editor asked us to clarify upfront exactly how this book was written, to explain "to the full satisfaction of the reader that these are indeed her words." I am happy to oblige.

This book took 10 years to write.

That time frame may best be appreciated by understanding the arduously slow progress involved. I communicate through facilitated communication (fc), which is a form of augmentative and alternative communication seen as a basic right by The Autism National Committee (AutCom), The Association for the Severely Handicapped (TASH) now The Association for Persons with Severe Handicaps, and me. FC users are supported by individuals called facilitators who provide physical support to help stabilize movement, reduce impulsive pointing and perseverations (repetition of the same motor response) and increase movement initiation.

The goal of facilitated communication (supported typing) is to progress toward independent typing. I work hard every day with several facilitators to accomplish that goal and now type with just one hand touching my back for support to help me initiate movement and overcome my apraxia. The National Institute of Health defines apraxia (called dyspraxia if mild) as a neurological disorder characterized by loss of the ability to execute or carry out learned movements despite having the desire and ability to perform them. This includes talking and typing. I also struggle with ataxia, which is characterized by imbalance, unsteady walk and tendency to stumble, problems with fine motor movements, and difficulty positioning in space. I often politely ask my brain to please move my hand to do this or that only to be told, "We're sorry due to high autism volume we are not able to answer your call at this time. Please try harder later." These vexations may prevent me from ever being a good driver, a great drunk driver sure, but never good. I am however determined to be the best writer I can be and this book is my Rubicon.

Our website features a library of videos and photos showing my gradual progression from hand over hand support to one hand touching my back. I invite you to view my technique at: http://www.muleandmuseproductions.com. For example, on the video, "First FC Day with Jeremy" it shows him supporting my wrist while we type common knowledge. Typing stuff we both know and expect is a great way to start practicing FC with someone new to get both people comfortable with the feel. If memory serves, and mine does very well and on my own I might add, the first day we typed the names of the seven dwarfs. The old joke, "a clear conscience is merely the result of a bad memory" fits me as badly as most professions other than being a writer as my conscience and memory are crystal clear and now both on display. From there, Jeremy weaned his support each day and we moved on to me typing information known only to me with him standing behind me and touching my back with his finger tips as seen on the clip "Solo Typing with Jeremy 2012".

Readers are also encouraged to learn the process from others like me from a variety of documentaries and films such as: 1. "Here We Are World: A Conversation Among Friends", 2. "Autism is a World", 3. "My Classic Life As an Artist: A Portrait of Larry Bissonnette, 4. "In My Language", 5.

"Kayla's Voice", 6. "Inside the Edge: A Journey to Using Speech Through Typing", 7. "Including Samuel", 8. "Educating Peter", 9. "Regular Lives", and 10. "Wretches and Jabberers".

Additional understanding of facilitated communication from researchers and practitioners can be found at Institute of Communication and Inclusion at Syracuse University where I and many others learned the standards for practice and have achieved the goal of facilitation, "namely independent typing and/or a combination of speaking and typing". The web site for the Institute of Communication and Inclusion at Syracuse University provides empirical data supporting the validity of the way I communicate. Two excellent summaries of such research can be found at: http://soe.syr.edu/centers_institutes/insitute_communication_inclusion/Research/authorship_and_controversy.aspx and http://soe.syr.edu/media/documents/2011/6/Research_Supporting_Authorship_version_22.pdf.

When I finally realized that it is easier to change me rather than everyone else, I put learning how to type on my own as priority number one. That focus resulted in hundreds of hours of practice and real improvement.

The first part of this book was written by me using hand over hand facilitated communication. A video of this level of support can also be seen on our web site's video library in the clip titled, "Hand Over Hand Support". The chapters in the second part of this book were written by me using progressively less support as seen in the photograph on the next page of me typing with elbow support from Dr. Dreke. Lois typed her chapters by herself, as she is less interesting.

Barb typing with elbow support from Dr. Dreke

Contents

Foreword

When Barb and Lois asked us to write the foreword to their book, we thought much about how to begin, what word(s) to use first. Friendship. This is a story, a life, a partnership, a journey grounded in friendship, connectedness. The reader is invited to consider the possibilities, challenges, joys, and pains that come along with choosing deep connectedness with others.

Connectedness. Barb and Lois take a risk in teaching us the pathway toward friendship. They show us that we are all puzzle pieces that, when connected, can learn from and be with one another in new and even unexpected ways. They show us also how to reenvision the very meaning of communication and learning—something we believe should be carefully considered by all practitioners and society at large. Connection is found in inviting new perspectives—something you will find by opening yourself up to this book. Read with care. Invite connection.

Friendship. We are both friends, former teachers, special educators by training. We began our friendship journey with both Barb and Lois in graduate school. We now work with preservice teachers. In the book, Barb mentions that it was her words that got our attention; really, it was not. It was who she was. Her person. We have learned not to demand, expect, need, depend upon, or even look for verbalness in our friends. We have learned, through Barb, that verbal and even written language is often overrated. It leads us to forget that connection is also found in *just being*. Those long and pleasant hours of sitting in quiet stillness with someone and knowing that you are learning how to be friends across language modalities—these are the moments we came to know Barb as our friend.

Indeed, we have always valued and learned much from her writing; yet, we would be remiss not to share that we have learned just as much (and probably even more) from learning how to be together away from the noise (both the written and verbal kind). As teachers trained to assess and categorize, Barb has taught us that the presumed connection between intelligence and verbal communication is a myth; a myth waiting to be unpacked and deconstructed by those willing to connect across differences. As you read the book, you will be invited to join in this unpacking. It is our hope that all teachers, especially those beginning their careers, read this book. Dispel the myths of intelligence of a certain kind as we stand face to face with our students. Connectedness, relating, and belonging. May we teach from the heart to the heart. The head will follow.

What we see in this book is the power of narrative—free-flowing storytelling, the kind that even breaks a few "rules." You, too, will find power, new insights, expectations, and ways of being in the world in the stream of stories rushing out of Lois' and Barb's hearts. Told in unexpected ways at times—even in ways in which the next story told is unexpected—the narrative calls to you. These stories invite you to wonder, cry, laugh, agree, disagree and/or question your own presuppositions. Stories call you to raw experience, experience unordained by pretext. Pure in their vulnerability. Naked friendship. Challenges unearthed and examined with a gentle eye to reconciliation and reconnection. At all times, the power of the narrative creates the very connections embodied in the title. We truly might be you.

Jessica Nina Lester, Ph.D., and Elizabeth Price, Ph.D.c
Independence Day, July 2012

Dedications

From Barb:
To Smother and Dad. She always wants the best for me and strives day after day, year after year, decade after decade to accomplish that. He loves me forever special. Grateful, B

From Lois:
To Ty and Elijah, whose gifts of unprecedented love teach me beyond what I am able to intellectually absorb, but not more than I can appreciate.

Chapter 1
Disguised as a Poor Thinker

I am Barb Rentenbach. One of my defining labels is autism—the severe kind, if I may be so bold. For decades, I bumped around this vexatious arcade of blaring impersonal voices, erratic assaults of color and light, undefined loneliness, and relentless confusion. Eventually, I let down my bulwark and discovered clarity, purpose, meaning, confidence, independence, and friends.

Today, I am at peace and happily productive. The paths to that state of being were filled with considerable pain, intense anger, frustration, and lots of trials and errors—and that is not the half of what my parents went through.

My unique design gives me receptive language, but expressive is primarily nonsensical. I say "primarily" because, like a broken watch being accurate twice a day, sometimes my inexorable stock phrases, like "You are not going," "Fire Truck," "It's raining," "You can't go to the pool," "Just a minute," "Pig," "Don't get in the mail truck," "She is not here," "No, Ma'am!" "Nice," "Oh, my God!" "The ballgame," "Damn it!" "I'm mad," "It's Dad's car," and my personal favorite, "It's mine, it's mine," are relevant.

Furthermore, my facial expressions did not always match my emotions. I can walk and move fairly well, but my fine motor skills are limited and my initiation impulse is extremely weak, so assistance is needed in almost every life sphere. My confusion, frustration, isolation, and anger often erupted without warning, putting any handy "normal" or myself in real danger of being kicked, bitten, hit, grabbed, and pinched. Plus, when I am feeling overwhelmed, I have this expensive and stupid habit of breaking my own glasses. Pricey, "indestructible" frames prove no match for ole Barb.

I don't look normal. I appear quite messed up and a prime candidate for nothing but pity and patronization, with a sprinkling of repulsion and fear.

I am disguised as a poor thinker.

I am writing this while a friend supports my forearm so my lifeline index finger hovers above an oversized keyboard. This process is called facilitated communication (FC) and freaks out a lot of people. Critics contend that the normal who supports the hand of the "abnormal" leads the typing and, therefore, fraudulently takes advantage of the clueless, disabled victim. I can only speak for myself and will continue to do just that. I am neither clueless, disabled, nor a victim.

The time has come for me to be my synergistic self and to no longer give thought effort to trying to convince others of my abilities. The questions will always be asked. I respectfully inform the curious and hurtful nonbelievers alike that my family and I have addressed the authorship issue already too many times to recall. The verdict is in—"Barb is in here." I will no longer use my precious, supported typing time to help others believe in me. If some people like my work and I touch lives, then I am contented. I will not be liked by, believed by, or touch everyone. That is true for all. I am no exception.

The numbers and letters on my keyboard are about two and a half times larger than standard. This helps a great deal for a couple of reasons. For one, I am as blind as a one-eyed cavefish. This has nothing to do with autism and everything to do with "shit happens." The big board also helps with one of my autistic-related challenges concerning motor control. It is very difficult to get my body—in this case my index finger—to do my mental biddings. When I move across this large board and spy the key I wish to strike down upon, I am less likely to hit more than one character.

I type with many people to communicate my needs and participate in conversation.

It should be noted that until age nineteen (1992), I was thought to be profoundly retarded. Facilitated communication changed that. If you must taste a little validation before my story is poignant, then I will briefly oblige. I type with the same vocabulary, knowledge base, lack of humility, irreverent sense of humor, impassioned opinions, and overused sarcasm no matter who supports my flailing appendage.

There is hope for all is my message. Allow me to share some accomplishments I was able to experience these past few years with the help of a well-synchronized support team, consisting of my educational psychologist, personal trainers, speech therapist, personal attendants, one-on-one academic tutors, normal roommates, and of course, my check-writing parents, who have been tireless in their commitment to help me lead the most rewarding and full life imaginable.

For one thing, I lost weight. Sure, that news flash may not make JAMA's cover story concerning autistic breakthroughs, but for this thirty-four-year old, previously pudgy American woman, it made a huge difference in confidence and motivation.

Each month, I am asked what two life-enhancing goals I would like to focus on. Weight loss was one of the ones I choose first. Now, if you knew what a train wreck I was when Lois Prislovsky, Ph.D., my educational psychologist, had me start all this, you would surely laugh out loud and proclaim, "Darlin', that ought to be the least of your worries"; if you hail from the South, others might simply question the logic of concentrating on minor outward appearances first. My point is Barb's opinion was heard.

In no particular order, let me give a grocery list of some of the recent progress: (1) shopping for purchasing and staffing my own condo (Prior to that, I lived either with my parents or in a group home for Special Forces members.); (2) eliminating most of my destructive and inappropriate behaviors (Here are a few examples. No kidding, my frustration-based aggression is almost completely eradicated. And I am pleased to report that I am much less likely to surreptitiously raid refrigerators or other unguarded food sources and gorge until I am physically numb and ill just for something to do in an attempt to fill an unquenchable hunger in my heart. Also, much to my ophthalmologist's chagrin, since his boat is not quite paid off, my "indestructible" spectacles have been in pristine condition for years.); (3) facilitating with many more people; (4) decreasing the typing support needed, from full hand encasement to elbow support (I can even type on my own with no support, but that takes tremendous effort and concentration on my part and the patience of Job on the audience's; (5) making nonpaid friends (for me unprecedented and priceless); (6) discovering and doing a career that I love—writing; (7) learning—I have done more thinking in each of the past five years than in the previous twenty-nine combined; (8) testing my IQ was finally done—it turns out I am not retarded...what a relief; (9) making noticeable gains by finally training my mouth muscles to allow me to articulate several handy words when appropriate; (10) smiling on cue and when I feel happy is now also possible; and (11) helping to create a nonprofit organization so that such dramatic, positive differences can be made in the lives of others like me.

Eavesdropping is more than a hobby for me—it is a way of life. One would be surprised how loose lipped and informative folks are when they consider themselves to be in the presence of a nonsentient being or, at the very least, someone they think is not capable of telling the tale. The array of knowledge gained from this indiscretion has yielded much. I honed my skills and am capable of laser-focusing my hearing to absorb murmured tidbits and side-mouthed conversations from across a crowded restaurant or from several rooms away.

I once overheard Lois say to a professional peer concerning our relationship, "I would choose to change nothing in my less-than-perfect past, because somehow the concoction of choices lead our lives and minds to intertwine. It is one of my deepest pleasures to know Barb well."

Eavesdropping has always helped me know where I stand with complicated normals.

I am blessed to be so appreciated. But my good fortune does not stop there. I am rich—and old money to boot.

No expense has been spared when it comes to this severely disabled daughter of the American republic. I want for nothing money can buy. However, my greatest wealth is my parents.

Mom and Dad have always been directly involved in every aspect of my care. Today, these long-suffering souls are my biggest fans and dearest friends. I am humbled by their ineffable generosity of self. Maybe it is because I am them— the product of themselves. Whatever the reason, Barbara and Mike Rentenbach unceasingly give love, time, sleep, bathing, wiping, feeding, clothing, toleration, teeth brushing, nose blowing, reading, researching, funding, prayer, understanding, and hope to little old me. They always have. If they felt Sisyphean about their parenting toil, I never picked up on it.

I don't know why I was allotted such a bounty in life, but I am convinced the time has come for me to make some major efforts and start giving back. I must live my adult life in earnest and show the investments of so many were not in vain. I trust writing will add some balance.

My mom, Smother, is quite the genealogist (I find the wealthy find comfort in historical validation.). Our family motto was, *Sola Virtus Invicta*—virtue alone invincible. I intend to honor that creed and undertake writing to share. Two ancestral poems written in Maryland in the 1600s bolster my resolve:

"Inarticulate" by Thomas Wells, Sr., (1680-1702): "Think of all the great thoughts locked in keen but inarticulate minds, struggling for expression, sure to die a-bornin' in clumsy speech and lost—forever."

"Experience" by Colonel Henry Ridgeley, Sr., (1625-1710): "The wisest old Philosopher has never found a substitute for Experience; let your Life's lessons be an open book, that all may read and wiser grow."

"Synergy" contains accounts of experiences with exclusion, confusion, and perception that I now know are neither mainstream nor the center of the universe. Session work with Lois is also sprinkled in to give a glimpse of who I am and how I got here. I hope my story and the accompanying practical implications assist others in finding their way and giving capacity.

Practical Implications

1. Providing alternative forms of communication for those who do not speak is as important as education gets.

2. Know miracles happen.

3. Look back with gratitude, look forward with fortitude, but for now, look for what you want to see and be her.

4. For fresh ideas on improving quality of life, continue reading.

Meet my makers, Mike and Barbara Rentenbach

Chapter 2

Twenty-Eight and Needing a Reason to Continue Living

Mom and Dad are tired—bone tired. My frazzled family can't hold together much longer with no hope or relief in sight. Mom is on the cusp of a nervous breakdown. Dad's only refuge is the office. Mom has no haven. I am mentally and physically with her twenty-four seven. I require constant supervision and can only communicate with Mom and Dad, and then only by crudely pointing to letters and pictures on a laminated board while they hold my hand firmly and provide backward resistance. I can type much more fluently with a handful of facilitators, but only one of those lives in Knoxville. She has three children, a traveling spouse, and a full-time job—and thus not a great deal of time to broker endless daily questions from dear Smother. You see, we were not well equipped for my return from Stewart Home.

Stewart Home is a residential community for adults with developmental disabilities. We are talking hundreds of retards. It was not a bad place. It was clean, well staffed, and had many planned activities to occupy the minds and bodies of the entrusted sheep. I rather liked being away from home for the first time. I made friends with a girl who *worked* there: Randy. We quickly became fluent with facilitation, so I got to speak my mind, go shopping, laugh, get massages, and do activities that interested me from time to time. I stayed at Stewart Home for five years. Unfortunately—or fortunately, I see now—my pal got busted for pot and fired. So that was the end of my five-year moratorium, during which I bothered the least number of people. "I am back." Surely, those words resonated in my

Mom's head like an ineluctable jingle. Mom's life would once again cease to be her own.

Returning home, I also felt the strain, as I had grown accustomed to being left alone. Mom is not for allowing idleness in her home. I was not left alone. And so, Mom and I began to make life full of tortuous demands on each other. I battled her petulant hovering with all manner of aggressive, manipulative, messy, infantile, feral, spoiled behaviors. Dad was pissed. I was making his outgoing, beautifully together wife a worn-out, babbling hag. He did not know what, but something had to be done and fast.

Dad is a practical, heavy-duty businessman. He owns a large construction and engineering corporation. The man knows how to hire the right professionals. He got headhunters on the case. Next thing you know, we had a family interview with a highly recommended specialist. Mom didn't even know what kind of respite to ask for. The smiling shrink (SS) mostly listened to fragmented thoughts, suggestions, and countless references to various organizations, theories, and previous support workers spitted out by my overwhelmed Mom. Dad was charming but very serious. The little candidate was under my Dad's most powerful microscope. I was more curious than I can ever remember. The clear little Tupperware bowl of nuts and bolts that I carried around and sifted for years sat undisturbed on my round lap, which rocked almost undetectably. I was so intrigued, I sat still and quiet for the entire two-hour meeting, which has never happened before or since. Well, turned out God was there, too. That day, the lives of all present, and then some, changed forever. Miracles began to occur one after another like gourmet cookies emerging from a stone kiln.

Next, I was to get to know the smiling shrink. The following Monday, we went on a solo mission to Wendy's fast-food restaurant, where I conducted many experiments on the eager young shrink. First, repulsion—would she be able to withstand the public embarrassment of dining with a growling Neanderthal who devoured both portions of cow? She did so with a genuine smile. Next, fear—would she run from the unpredictable grabs by a larger, more menacing creature? No, the optimistically warped doctor misinterpreted my offish assails as a friendly yet awkward closeness gesture. The most substantial test would take significantly more patience on my part. I will outlast her momentary interest by evading progress. I have outlasted the best of them. This well-intentioned do-gooder will soon retreat from my world and I can resume my comfortable solitude.

With any luck and decent manipulative creativity on my part, I will be safely tucked away in a posh home for institutionalized types by summer. That way, everybody wins. Mom and Dad are guilt-free and can get some rest and golf a bit. The smiling shrink (SS) gains some well-needed experience with incorrigibles and gets paid for her troubles. And me—well, I can survive. No need to thrive. My mind is not a bad place to live. Who knows, I might even find another pot-smoking friend to help me pass the time.

Well, you could have knocked me over with a worm of floating light (like the ones seen drifting across one's visual field while staring into an overcast sky) when I felt myself enjoying her lively company so much.

A week into our work, our sessions were as welcome and revitalizing as that first gulp of air finally sucked in after pushing through perfectly chlorinated water just prior to my lungs exploding from toying with living submerged permanently. I considered postponing my fancy institutional quest a while longer while I explored the depths of this new worker. This might amuse me for some time. The thing simply got out of hand.

After a few more weeks, the smiling shrink started bringing in even more interesting, attractive, caring, and smiling people. They were all eager to work one-on-one with crazy me. How could I go back into my brain now, with all of this enticing action centered on me—a hedonist's dream come true? I will come out and play for a while. If my happy crew becomes demanding, I can always delve into the extreme and find my way back to some peaceful sanitarium. Meanwhile, let's see what they've got.

When asked what productive goal I wanted to tackle first, I typed, "fat be gone." Tah-dah, two handsome male graduate students will work out with me for six hours a week in the University of Tennessee campus, alongside some of the most athletic and beautiful people in the world. So far, so good.

I lost weight quickly. I wanted to look good. With the weight off and thinking I was reasonably pretty, I actually started to be interested in men. My first victim was babe Avery—my blond, blue-eyed beefcake personal trainer. Such a crush sounds perfectly normal, but there is a twist—there's always a twist with Barb. You see, involvement was not my intention. I was in the midst of planning my probable final escape from this far-too-complicated world and then, bang—all of a sudden I am being cajoled into significant participation.

My odd observer life was evaporating. The draws were gradual but powerful. I was actually starting to want to make the painful efforts needed to be a less parasitic being, because the rewards of participation are starting to outweigh the serenity and ennui of my own world, which consists only of my wacky neuronal firings.

Of course, my first crush bore no fruit, as I was still Helen Keller before her water epiphany. I was starting to care, and the problem with making such a leap at twenty-eight is the catch-up work is monumental. My parents and the support team seemed to be up for the task. My question was, would Barb have the stamina? God, I hoped so. The distinction is that previously, my progress stagnated because of my own lack of commitment to any real change that would be perpetually taxing. Being an unemployed, nonverbal rich girl can be quite luxurious and relatively stress free, especially with a get-out-of-jail-free card like autism.

What if I get invested in the outer world and make a real effort to be included and still fail to be successful at the level I desire? Then I am screwed, because the good normals will know that I am rather capable even if I am not terribly interesting or bright. That brings on a lifelong barrage of menial demands. Such chores are not worth fighting through the autistic noise to accomplish.

I am not the ambitious or adventurous type, but I have decided to bet the autistic farm on designing and creating the perfect life. I go now into the wild, wild world of normals.

Practical Implications

1. Give us the benefit of the doubt. Don't assume mental retardation based on behavior and poor communication. One has nothing to lose by assuming competence and treating the different person with nonpatronizing respect. Give us the freedom to rise to expectations…surpassing may come next.

2. Get to know us. That should be the first order of business—not trying to fix or change us. Let the autistic person know that you are here for them and want to get to know who they are and what they do. Everybody has this knowledge about self, although most have it hidden

under a bushel. Autistics traditionally have huge bushels weighting down their heads. It is challenging, but all are capable of discovering who they are and what they do. Let it shine.

3. Listen. With nonverbal or echolalic autistics, this seems daunting, but break it down. To listen means to make an effort to hear, take notice of, or heed. So, if folk are not talking or typing—observe. Study their past, proclivities, and how they spend their time. Find out what gives them joy. Once at least one interest is pinpointed, go from there and make learning opportunities and socialization related to that interest. For me, I was interested in history, science, and philosophy. I actually typed that fact many years ago, but that information was enough to get the ball rolling. Through books on tape and reading aloud, my curiosity came alive. Next, we slowly incorporated me discussing the readings with Lois or a tutor. To discuss, I had to type, so that increased my mental "on-task time," communication skills, and reason to roll out of bed.

4. Motivate. Motivation is often tricky for autistics. Curiosity jump-started my internal motivation rather than a burning desire to accomplish. Make participating in things outside of the autistic mind interesting, safe, and low-stress. Once you entice us out of the autistic mental house, we may find something worth visiting regularly.

5. Smile. Smiling is not wasted on autistics. We sense and often take on the affect of those around us. People who are happy, confident, honest, energetic, and don't take

themselves too seriously help make mentally external tasks appealing to us. SS insisted that my team members work with me in only short blocks of time like two or three hours to ensure "freshness." Burned-out, tired, listless, disingenuous, or pessimistic workers were not hired. Concerning the nickname, "smiling shrink" (SS), I gave Lois, I know she is an educational psychologist and not a psychiatrist or "shrink," but I find the moniker humorous and descriptive so it remains in my repertoire of hyperbole.

6. Be patient. What normals perceive as "waiting" and "wasting time," we may view as stasis. Like well-seasoned Tibetan monks, we are in no rush. We understand the reality of impermanence. We understand the reality that nothing is as it appears to be. Please, consider here my hypothesis that there are more autistics now because of human evolution. Autism may serve to provide the individual time and space to contemplate and meditate more so than any convent or monastery. Nonverbals "waste no time" on vows of silence. We simply live it.

7. Persevere. Set specific short—and long-term goals. Each day, do at least one thing designed to make progress towards one short-term and one long-term goal. Keep a detailed account of precisely what was accomplished each day. Review this log at the end of each month.

Dad dancing with his favorite Stewart Home inmate

Chapter 3

Horse and Rider

Synergy is one of the most fundamental and constant laws of the universe. We benefit from it every hour of our being. Every concept is a product of synergy. A designed beauty of synergy is that it serves only to add, never subtract. By definition, it means that the combined interaction of parts creates an effect greater than the sum of the parts. Individuals are the parts. I'm an odd little part.

I am a poster child for synergy. I am designed to aid in making evident the implicit need for a group effort in order to yield maximum returns.

Synergy is the byproduct of giving. Without synergistic support from normals – say, if I were simply warehoused—I would end up merely consuming resources. With a little help—okay, a lot of help—from connected normals—I may add to our collective body of knowledge, perspectives, and insights that have receded from the working memory of many.

One can ride synergy like an experienced surfer. Get yourself in position to become one with the others going that way, then stabilize on the board of gifts and joyously surf the empowered molecules rushing to shore. Swimming in by yourself takes much more effort and generates a less blissful rush. Plus, it is not nearly as cool. Taking credit for how beautifully you arrived at a destination shore is heresy. The whole point of making synergized results so beneficial is that it is an incentive program.

It is in our best interest to remember that we are all the same. People are flecks of God. Each God fragment dispersed through space-time has a slightly different shape. One shape is not superior to another. All are necessary to complete the perfect, infinite, God puzzle. To be proud that one "tolerates" diversity is ludicrous. The whole system is the sum of its parts. Be your part. Connect with other parts and the God puzzle is revealed.

With present-moment clarity, I recall when I recognized my part. My shape was reflected in the eyes of a friend.

I was twenty-eight years old and a few months into my work with SS when the happy crew of normals rallied to help me become more of a person. You see, in Western culture, significant people live outside of their minds. As the homeless are at a disadvantage because they must directly weather storms, cold, heat, and myriad dangers, those of us who exist invisibly in the conscious dream country of our minds suffer similar prejudices because we hardly exist in the external world and are therefore not censused.

I was working out; typing with others; looking for a condo distant enough from Smother to discourage drop-ins and drive-bys but close enough to ensure comfort; studying history, current events, science, philosophy, and literature with personal tutors; and taking general education diploma (GED) practice tests (It seems my special education high school diploma was so "special" that it is not worth the paper it is written on.). All this was designed to help me reach the societal personhood goals I listed: lose weight, live on my own, take college classes, and have nonpaid friends.

The devil was in the details. Like a rehabilitated, housed, and newly employed former street person who longs for the freedom of time, accountability, spontaneity, and inebriation – I regressed. My mental cardboard box beckoned me to shut the flaps and cover up with rags, when I realized the daily concerted effort involved in living in a system run by others. I came to a screeching halt.

SS and I were at Pellissippi State Community College in a private study room. She had me plugging away, answering banal multiple-choice questions based on a poorly written war poem, when I hit a snag. None of the choices were correct. I knew I was right about this. I pushed the board away and put my head down on the grimy desk. It smelled of too many hands and impregnated my mind with an olfactory experience that could not be shaken. That smell permeated everything invisible that I held dear. My whole brain was pickled with that insidious odor. I could think of nothing else except maybe glimpses connotated with that smell, like my pudgy white knuckles wrapped around the wooden horn of a carousel unicorn or an eight-pound purple, swirled bowling ball two inches away from my face. I was unable to recall how my mind smelled prior to this invasion. I lost control of my internal environment.

I am inured to always having precious little power outside of my head. But the thought of losing my boss status inside was terrifying. I reconsidered my gamble of making the effort to come out in the world to get a piece of the pie, because I feared losing my internal bread and butter.

I was in danger of losing more than my novice personhood. I was in danger of becoming nothing. Something had to be done.

I refused to type. I considered never communicating again with anyone. I did not see the point. I did not know I was a writer then and did not realize the oily, germy smell was simply a preservation that would evaporate when I led my autism into an agreed-upon arena of remission.

Day after day, SS kept bringing me to the same work area, where she would inform me that this was my time and she was there for me. Then she would shut up and be there for me.

For an hour each day, SS literally stood beside my chair with her mind and hands open to me. Every five minutes or so, I would raise my bobbling head and grab her waiting hand. I demonstratively struck the "No" rectangle on the board. My laconic plan was nebulous. I will wait it out. She will go away. I will make her mad and that should be interesting to watch. Who knows where this will lead? I know I can last longer – that I can control, smell of too many hands or not.

Her plan was clear but unproven. SS sought to find out who resides in this ill-wired human and help me become that.

I could tell they did not teach her that in school, because SS was too eager and pleased with the beauty of the process. She was delighted to be trying something new. This information was easy to intercept. Most bright people have at least some level of code that I must first decipher in order to gather any juicy intelligence when I mind squat, but not SS. She is so simple that at first I thought she was stupid. Her mental vestibule is not primitively fortressed. It is an open bay window. I am now better at spotting bay window types. Jimmy Carter, for example, is a man who was too honest to make an effective president. I recall hearing that when asked if he ever cheated on his wife, he said, "Only in my mind." Probity may profoundly impair politics. The shape does not fit. In time, Jimmy Carter's piece was turned another way and revealed. The configuration fit the God puzzle perfectly. In fact, it was a corner piece and earned a Nobel Peace Prize.

Somewhere near the end of week two of my silent filibuster, shape was revealed.

SS touched my shoulders and fluffed my hair, as I allow her to do on occasion, and she spoke with moist, God-filled eyes that I immediately recognized as my own. I still play back those words when I wish to center and smile: "Don't you see? Don't you know that you and I are the same? You are I and I am you. And when the tables are turned, as they often are, you are there for me."

With my *Sesame Street* understanding of quantum physics, I put it all together. All creation is made of the same continuously form-changing stuff. Nothing separates anything or anyone. Space separating the pieces is impermanent and not the best practice. That was when the fun began.

I did not immediately come to external attention and profoundly type the day away. I was too captivated. A rivulet of the haunting "too many hands" smell slinked out of my mental house. At that moment, I intuited, "I am a writer." I did manage to utter, "K, k, k" (translated for normals as "Okay"). I did not hit the "No" rectangle. SS was content with my turn toward the positive and began to cheerfully pack up. "Time," she said. "Tomorrow we should work on some desensitization strategies and cognitive therapy steps to help you work through this block."

That night under my comforter, where my best thinking is done, I began working on a split custody agreement. The imbroglio was this: I am a writer and a mute autistic. That is an unusually shaped piece. No wonder I never fit when just the autistic part was crammed in. My writer protrusions must be considered or this will never work. To be a successful writer, I must come out and communicate with others. To be a fulfilled autistic, I must never stray far from my rabbit hole.

Autism is not a place or a disability. It is a realm of existence – a personal, parallel universe. I don't go there. I am there.

Autism is who I am and what I do—just as a writer is who I am and what I do. What happens in autism usually stays in autism.

There is no gravity, sure footing, people, indigenous tongue, work product, or linear time. It is wondrous yet filled with terrifying land mines activated by friction from neighboring universes. Touch and taste populate its vastness. Sounds dominate the house, smells rule the senate, and visuals not originating from the eyes top its polydimensional hierarchy. These senses overlap in a way that outlander normals have rarely considered. I will not take the time to elaborate here but will simply introduce this teaser to be described at length in another chapter. In autism, I see, smell, hear, taste, and feel color. Music performs even more sensory manifestations. And movement? Well, let's just say I am well traveled without ever physically leaving the room. And that, my friends, is better than cable.

Autism is busy but not hectic, as the absence of linear time makes patience part of the breathable atmosphere. Variations in senses create seasons and storms. Autism is inhospitable to outlanders. The perpetual ungrounded hullabaloo is too confusing and loses everything in translation.

Autism is not self-sustaining. No food, water, shelter, or waste management systems exist and are rarely even considered, because that requires purposeful work. Autism generates sensory experiences, perceptual interpretations, and exhaustive contemplation of minutiae—not work products.

At first glance, autism's relationship to the world appears parasitic. I now straddle both realms and seek to disprove the hypothesis that autism needs the world but the world does not need autism. The trick is not to coexist as autism and a writer but to synergistically be my whole self. It was time to broker a deal.

Autism is not formless, but outlander words fail me in describing its constitution. So, for the purpose of this negotiation, autism has chosen to be represented as a horse with Herculean senses, otherworldly proclivities, and a preference for the simple life. The writer is a petite jockey who, without an inexorable steed, is essentially powerless in the world of normals. Autism wants to run fast and free through rolling hills of lights, colors, rhythms, textures, tastes, tones, odors, and timeless meditations with no demands or interference. The jockey wants a chance to compete and become significant in the world.

The jockey loves and respects this horse. When high atop this formidable creature, the jockey has a unique perspective and becomes empowered and inspired. Few have been able to ride this kind of mythical stallion successfully in the world. The jockey is careful not to tame autism, because that tempers its power. The key is channeling autism's bursts to explode on the world track, catapulting horse and rider in the same direction. Channeling should be brief and the steed should be rewarded soon after with unbridled field time. As in any settlement, cooperation and a predictable structure are vital.

Here was the proposed schedule. First thing in the morning, the horse is called in from the fields, where it has been doing its own thing since late afternoon the previous day. The horse is led to an arena, where it is contained but untethered. Its basic needs are met. Nearby, the jockey is milling about the world by taking care of the daily business, mundane household duties, exercising, and learning more of the trade. Then, at the same time each day, the jockey reins in the horse from the paddock. Jockey and horse become one and ride hard.

The run is sublime. Synergy generates a perfect puzzle piece. Horse and rider fit in, touch others, and fulfill their part. When horse and rider are spent, they buckle away from the puzzle and fade to an awkward gallop. The jockey quickly dismounts. The jockey knows better than to mount too long. Bucking, biting, and kicking will ensue if the chomping horse is not allowed to take to the fields solo as agreed.

Well, that is one way to explain how I exist happily and successfully as an autistic and a writer. The aforementioned parable is accurate but sanitized. I really do follow such a schedule, which allows blocks of "pseudo on" states where I am in the world—eating, drinking, exercising, listening, and learning—but am paddocked and essentially undisturbed (I am not expected to type during these times. Typing requires my "full on" resources.). Also built into my days is significant chill time when I am not required to interact or perform at any level, which allows me to refuel and frolic in my field. But for two hours each day, between the paddock and the field, I synergize my efforts and identities and write. I am most alive and fully on at these times, because that is who I am and what I do.

The arrangement works. However on occasions one world bleeds over into the next—unannounced. This usually creates problems, but not always. Sometimes, unprecedented experiences are generated. For example, about one and one-half years after this custody agreement was implemented, I had my first people dream. There are no people (well, no talking significant people) in my autism in either its conscious or unconscious lanes. So imagine my surprise when a dream starring people and words seeped in.

In my dream, SS was in some sort of abstract accident and lost her ability to speak. Of course, I visited the hospital immediately to take in such a sight. She typed. As usual, SS was in good spirits. I pecked away on my board and asked about her well-being, primarily to satisfy our caring audience of family and friends gathered to gawk and pay homage to the downed human. I knew she was fit as a Stradivarius, because I had camped out in her brain space for the better part of the day. After the cursory exchange, SS sat up and typed, "Let's make mute jokes." I was the first to indulge and typed, "Two mutes walk into a bar. The first typed, 'Heineken please.' The second ordered Guinness—room temperature. A domestically polluted patron belched, 'What are two mutes like you doing in a place like this?' The mutes simultaneously typed, 'The karaoke bar was closed.'"

Unscheduled realm overlaps are usually not so tidy. Being a writer means being an open book, so permit me to share one of the most unbecoming aspects of who I am. I literally cannot even wipe myself.

Chimpanzees use leaves to wipe their bottoms, but not ol' Barb. Apparently, that 98.6 percent where they are genetically identical to humans gave chimps an edge over me, who has yet to have my genes quantified. But when something is out of whack and my universes collide—it gets worse. I smear and taste my own feces. There—I said it.

As you can imagine, that was one of the biggie problems SS was employed to help me overcome. She even considered bringing in a behavior specialist who was a self-proclaimed and well-published expert in the area. At first, I couldn't believe some psychologist would specialize in such a bizarre and vile ritual as feces smearing and tasting, but it is apparently more common than I thought. We decided to try getting a handle on it ourselves before bringing in the shit doctor.

SS tried to make the cease-and-desist process seem logical to me, but first, she had to get me thinking and talking about it, which I had refused to do for decades because of humiliation. I want to be perceived as an intelligent, thoughtful adult, and smearing is hard to tie into that. "Hello, my name is Barb and I am a smearer." No, my filthy vice is not like alcoholism or other addictions. It is more disgusting. Outlanders will not understand. SS, an overenthusiastic proponent of forthrightness, disagreed.

Lois had me read Anne Lamott's, *Traveling Mercies,* where the author candidly talks about her bulimia, drunkenness,

sexual promiscuity, and her flabby thighs (which she calls
Aunties). Her style was open, humorous, warm, and bright. I
loved the book and respected her humanness. Lamott presented
her whole self as a well-developed character—a composite of
the good and the bad. SS convinced me that such disclosure
were not only therapeutic and made good tender for sound
writing but were also the best way to reduce the shame. I
embraced that logic because, if I was the one highlighting the
flaw, it disarms others who may seek to divulge my filthy
secret. Also, I find myself attracted to writers and others who
don't take themselves too seriously. I don't think people who
take themselves too seriously would announce such a gross
proclivity. Plus, self-deprecating humor is almost always a
lock. I agreed to discuss the subject because I understood it to
be the best way to gain power over it. I do not want to be a
smearer.

Lois: "Start with the antecedents to the behavior."

Barb: "Sadist, I take it you want me to tell you what
happens before I literally smear feces all over
myself and my luxury condo?"

Lois: "Please."

Barb: "Christina (personal attendant and roommate at the
time) and Smother are right. I usually partake in this
glamorous activity after my workout when I am
finally back at my condo haven and about to clock
out. I am off work. As you know, sadist junior,
formally known as sweet Brandon, is having me do
more sit-ups than Janet Jackson. It must be some
type of national contest among personal trainers.
Perhaps sadist junior will win a lifetime supply of
weight gainer. (Brandon, aka "Slim," is six-foot-

five and 155 pounds of smiling, enthusiastic, and easygoing personality.) I return home a weak woman with peristalsis to beat the band. Then I get on the toilet, also known as mistake number one. Number two comes next and is quite the pun.

"I try to wipe, and my extremities mock by brain's polite request. On a good day, with no physical exhaustion, my arms and hands comply, say, 75 percent of the time. Normally, I ask my arms and hands to stay clear of the shit. Because no matter how much I long to be more self-sufficient that day, I know attempting to wipe myself will only result in health department violations. Best send in the royal wipers.

"I must say that my man, Stephen Hawking, must have similar staffers makes me feel less ashamed; however, I can't imagine Dr. Hawking could be much of a smearing threat with that overworked, little left paw.

"Anyway, since this is an unscheduled BM (Did I mention how much we autistics are slaves to structure?), wipers are not on standby: I am left to my own poorly wired devices. I try to check on the status of my bowel movement, but my outer-world logic is fading fast because my battery is too low. I need to recharge in autism (Translation: I need "chill time.") I can't get there fast enough. My autism way of doing things overrides, and I depend on touch, taste, and smell to know a real-world object. By the time my BM is complete, my body is on autopilot. I am safe and sound in autism. Follow the soiled trail and you will find body and autism nestled beneath my comforter and sheets."

Lois: "What happens next?"

Barb: "I am completely disjointed at this point, and calling me in is difficult. What happens next depends on discovery timing. If my crime is discovered in the morning, I am better equipped to handle the consequences. No crime goes unpunished, but if I am roused before energy and clarity return, the cleanup process is much more drawn out, because my language understanding is retarded and my movements are slow and awkward, because my invisible staff are drunk in autism.

"Either way, I wake up to an agitated personal attendant who shuttles me to forced cleaning with stern, loud, direct supervision. I am commanded to strip and will remain naked until everything is clean. She hands me chemicals, scrubbing brushes, moist towels, abrasive sponges, or whatever is needed to restore the world to order. I help with laundry, tolerate hostile teeth brushing, and take a shower. Since I prefer baths, I must take showers for the rest of the week for complete restitution."

These days, smearing rarely happens. Maybe, twice a year I mess up. Consequences did not put an end to perhaps my most unbecoming habit. I have suffered punishments and consequences before. Finding purpose is what changed things.

I think the bulk of disturbing behaviors—like smearing, kicking, biting, grabbing, hitting, pica, manipulating tantrums, running away, stealing food from other's plates, handling objects for hours on end, breaking my glasses, etc.—have all melted away because none of those things serve my purpose.

All creatures are built to do more than survive. Quality of life requires it and life is designed to be quality. I must have instinctively known this and was therefore frustrated and angry to the core at doing nothing but passing time between here and autism. Those unsettling feelings and squandered energy manifested in bad behaviors.

My recent adult tutoring has taught me that a brain gains meaningful form by being plugged into context by having tasks it must strive to perform. This makes sense. Birds sing not because they have to but because they can, as it is part of their purpose and who they are. Birds strive to sing. They will sing whether or not anyone is around to hear, but trust me, they are all heard. Words are my notes and sentences are my songs. I strive to write. I trust others will enjoy and be lifted by the work, but I will continue to sing either way.

Not long after my purpose was revealed, I began to take responsibility as a writer. I considered myself gainfully employed. I learned about being a writer and started doing stuff writers do. I set a work schedule, developed production goals, researched, learned vocabulary, read, attended conferences, and developed correspondences with other writers, thinkers, and editors. It was another year before I was published. I communicate with many different people supporting my hand through the technique of facilitation. But that is talking, not writing. Professional writing I only do with Lois. Yes, I work hard to do my part, but the product you read is a result of true synergy.

Words are but puffs of imagination until Lois and I share them and shape them in the direction we mutually choose to go.

It is impossible to tag ownership to any particular sentence because Lois and I do not allow that even in our own minds. We are quite cognizant of how pride, ego, and "mine" dilute synergy. So, don't ask, "Who thought of that?" because we honestly don't know or care.

Perhaps, the best I can do is to convey our general constitutional makeups, and you, then, are free to ponder origins. SS and I have different worldviews. She is primarily a participant and I am an observer. Please don't waste too much time and energy on that wispy enigma of personal paradigms, as I think you may get the same kind of headache that comes from trying to figure out how two parts of oxygen combines with one part hydrogen to make wet.

You see, the writings you taste are made from ingredients of me synergizing the parts of myself (i.e., horse and rider). Others going that way blended in to make this cake. When Lois promised to help me become a writer, we both gave each other what we had to give. We did more than share. We gave each other our minds, thoughts, time, readings experiences, dreams, education, relationships, ancestors, energy, spiritual connections, and complete trust. I set out to become my writer self. Lois did not. Synergy worked exponentially, as it always does, and we became writers, nonpaid friends, advocates for others longing for purpose, rich with potential, and quite happy. This cake would have never been baked if it were not for autism—which brings us back to the question of whether or not the world is better off with or without autism. I know that it is better with.

I think autism is a valuable part of human evolution.

Consider the stagnation of our predecessors. *Homo erectus,* who existed for over a million years with basically only axe-like tools, hunting, and the use of fire. No significant technological, ritual, or symbolic improvements were made until *Homo sapiens* appeared about one hundred thousand years ago. *Homo sapiens* had something *Homo erectus* did not—language, grammatical, articulate, and referential speech. Language changed the world.

Modern humans became the sole survivor of a complex family tree because language allowed consciousness of our pasts, our futures, and ourselves. Innovations promoting surviving and thriving exploded. "Life can only be understood backwards, but it must be lived forwards," said Soren Kiekegaard.

These days, no human is equipped to process all the sensory and intellectual information available. Information overload is prevalent. Maybe autism is an evolutionary variation kite, flown to see if such a human wiring tweak will better equip us to deal with and process infinite information.

Research confirms that documented cases of autism and related spectrum disorders are increasing at unprecedented rates. Autistic tendencies may enable some humans to better weed out time perceptions and social/emotional/external distractions, which may hamper observations needed for specific problem solving. How often do normals take the time to really touch, smell, taste, hear, and truly observe a seemingly common object or parcel of nature?

Or perhaps, prevalent autistic characteristic, such as "language problems," may be the precursors to other forms of valid, consistent human communication, which are faster and more efficient and honest than speech. Please consider that before language became dominant, surely a minority of humans hard-wired for verbal speech existed and were probably also viewed as "different." Skull remains reveal that these individuals who became known as *Homo sapiens* even looked different, as their face was flatter, which allowed for articulate speech. These are a couple of the many reasons why I have great reservations about genetic engineering and cloning.

God's system of heredity depends on variation. History has shown that when we start tying to eliminate diversity, nature answers cruelly. Take, for example, the self-important royals who inbred to keep the royal blood pure. How many short-lived, hemophiliac retards with big ears (kidding) did that produce?

Can one imagine a world where humility was bred out? Consider who would clone. It would be those same white folks who now spend thousands of dollars each year on infertility treatments just so little Johnny is like them. Meanwhile, tiny, beautiful babies of color and special needs can't get adopted to literally save their life. My own incredibly smart and supportive mom would have probably chosen the cloning option if given the choice of that or having a special needs daughter destined to take a lifetime of care and countless resources. Imagine—she could play golf with a younger version of herself. Heaven—until Mom pulled every muscle trying to compete. See, cloning can even result in severe muscle strain.

Normals are often pleased with themselves and think they have a good handle on the past and a sound plan for the future, all the while participating with frenzy in the present. My own SS schedules people, places, events, work, leisure, and even passion in endless back-to-back "time" chunks. Her mind incessantly prioritizes these responsibilities and happenings based on a scale made up by normals. She hurries through or skips countless meals and other life joys in order to accomplish. I, on the other hand, have a lovely lunch every day, followed by a relaxing swim or fulfilling amount of peaceful chill time. I focus on one life concept at a time. I am not designed for physical or mental juggling. The outer world seems to value harrowing juggling acts. This autistic has a different perspective. Who is happier and closer to God: a napping native with a warm sun, clean ocean, and plenty of tasty trout, or a chainsaw juggler in a business suit with a buzzing cell phone?

I encourage all to discover your own shape, connect with others, and enjoy your lunch. The result will be resplendent and quite worth doing.

Practical Implications

1. Discover—Find out who the person is and help him or her to become the highest version of that.

2. Persevere—Don't give up. This may take years. Encourage all involved to enjoy and appreciate the process as much as the product.

3. Remember—We are all the same.

4. Understand—"Unbridled field time" refers to what I call "chill time." Allow the autistic person substantial time each day to be inside his or her autism. Make this be a regular time he or she can count on to be undisturbed. It is equally important to have inclusive external-world activities also scheduled. A well-rounded autistic needs both. We want to know what to expect and what to look forward to.

5. Open—Keep an open mind. Consider other forms of communication as potentially valid.

6. Empower—To the greatest extent possible the autistic person should have choices and decision-making power, especially concerning his or her schedule, staff, learning, and goals. Offer us responsibility and we may take it.

Facilitator/tutor Renee and me on the steps of my new condo with a freshly published article. I feel like George Jefferson – "moving on up".

Chapter 4
Barbara Ruth

"Barbara Ruth is sad, sad, sad. She is the retarded Rentenbach girl. Money can't fix what plagues this child." Carolyn whispered, "Autism. And she's got it bad. She can't talk. This kid barely feeds herself, and Lordy, what a putrid mess that is. She is damn near grown now and can't even wipe herself. And, buddy, watch out—that one is mean as a hornet. She bites, kicks, pinches, grabs, and terrorizes her parents, teachers, and students, too. They can't leave her alone for a second. She runs off," Carolyn tells her walking buddy as they spy their neighbor trying to walk on the same Lakeshore track with disturbed daughter in tow, ululating a fierce nonhuman wail, perhaps something in a wounded dolphin's repertoire. As thin, rich, perpetually tanned Mrs. Carolyn spoke these words without a breathing pause, she smiled and waved to Mom, who was safely out of earshot.

My name is Barb. I am the Rentenbach girl, but I am not the retarded one—Barbara Ruth. She is gone—she left over a year ago. Folks have no idea I can hear like a long-eared hare at dusk. Truth is, most wouldn't have cared anyway, because they think I am a black hole—what goes in, never comes out. Their cruel secrets aren't safe with me. This safety deposit box is about to blow wide open for all the world to see.

I am nineteen years old and just returned from Syracuse, New York, where my parents met my mind for the first time in seventeen years. I'd had an early debut, but then, just before I turned two, my humanity went into hibernation.

Thinking ceased to build upon itself. That is when Barbara Ruth filled in for me and went into survival mode. Each moment was a confusing ambush, and she sought only to gulp the next breath of fleeting clarity. Words changed all that, and my parents bought those in upstate New York. It was a sweet purchase—two for one: words and a daughter with a working mind.

The deal is, I still can't talk, but I can type on a keyboard or letter board if someone supports my wobbly hand. The process is called facilitated communication, or "assisted typing." It is quite controversial, meaning lots of people think it is not really me doing the typing. This infuriates me, and I considered chucking the whole thing out of spite. But the words...the words possessed me.

Letters first became formidable and gave me power and glimpses of humanity. I touch "Y" and, tah-dah, Mom knows I do want to go swimming, or let me go towards "N," and what I want to stop or not happen magically yields to my power.

Then combine letters, like they have been forever singing and showing at school, and words appear and take the place over. Words are everything: life, death, colors, foods, people, places, wants—everything in the past, present, and future.

I like the pseudo-concrete nature of it all. Words are stable. You can count on them.

My inner world became an obsessive-compulsive's dream closet. All knowledge, experiences, original ideas, facts, feelings, and identities were neatly labeled, categorized, and stacked for easy access and use. Before words, if my mental closet was opened to the outside world, even a crack, the jumbled, nondescript contents with sharp edges exploded out. The chaos painfully disrupted both worlds. Words and sentences now make it possible to come out of the closet. Who or what will emerge?

Barbara Ruth, the what, vanished. All that remains is Barb, who is slightly disoriented from hitting the hibernation snooze far too often, but she is up and out nevertheless. Justice is on my mind

One of my first orders of business as Barb is to reveal the contents of the box.

My thoughts revolve only around me. I assume that is the way things work—although I wonder how this great big world can remain cohesive if all inhabitants dwell only on their own situations. Perhaps they are all thinking of me, too? I am not stupid; I know this is called "egocentrism" and it is not becoming for a lady to be so openly self-centered. I don't care. After seventeen years of silence, I have no intention of editing to assuage an unjust world.

I will not be dismissed. Barbara Ruth was dismissed and considered by no one except her obligated parents whom God outfitted with the patience of Tibetan sand artists and serious money: heavy-duty equipment for a Herculean battle. Countless caretakers were paid to consider Barbara Ruth and give respite to her frontline battle-fatigued parents.

In fact, Barbara Ruth did not even consider her own self, as even the most general classification was too uncertain. She had no frame of reference and certainly no pronoun labels for whatever concoction constituted "Barbara Ruth."

She was bombarded with too much free-floating information to logically rule out categories, and I had no method for keeping track of new learning. I am glad she is gone. This world was no place for Barbara Ruth.

I am not even sure this world is ready for Barb, but I am here nonetheless.

Elke is a German grad student hired by my parents to give my mom a tending break and to take me where I am expected. I use this sound-minded normal to convey my thoughts.

Elke is a bright, no-nonsense kind of girl and she supports me while I type. She thinks I am a spoiled brat and tells me so on every occasion when the thought scampers across her all-or-nothing brain.

The good news is that while she may disagree with my endless demands and rants, Elke always allows me to type what I want to say with no editing. Elke does this for several reasons. One is that she is too honest for her own good and feels it is her duty to help me type my mind no matter how destructive or hurtful my sentiments. Also, new immigrants are real zealots when it comes to the First Amendment. But, I think the main reason is Elke feels I must learn from my own mistakes. This is accompanied by her sadistic glee when my undiplomatic princess decrees shotgun out and I suffer consequences such as more alienation and lack of freedom.

I type with other people, too, but Elke is my primary facilitator because she lives with us.

The first thing I told my attentive parent was to stop dressing me like Barbara Ruth the retard. My German took me shopping, and now I look pretty good for an overweight adolescent with chewed-off, warty fingernails and skin scabby from a hearty does of psoriasis, puffed up and often bleeding from incessant picking stimulation.

Other than clothes and myriad stylistic and taste preferences, the main thing released from the box was anger.

Many find this odd, since Barbara Ruth also raged about a good bit of the time, so anger was not much of a secret. But there is a difference. Barbara Ruth's anger and aggression were fueled by fear and loss of options—a cornered lame fox at the close of a hunt. I am angry at you normals because you have the world by the tail but don't allow your pious selves to see yourselves in me. You veil my personhood. Barb is mad, mad, mad.

I retrieve a file on the matter to better explain. Once I got the hang of literacy, I acquired the habit of performing class work mentally.

The following is a speech I wrote but never delivered. I was never called upon. Some things never change, even when miracles happen and the mute communicate.

The truth is I wasted a great deal of angst and a pound of picked flesh worrying about my increased schoolwork load that never came. I assumed I would have to start studying, taking tests, and being called on in class now that they knew I could learn and communicate. My days of being an eyesore, state-mandated recliner to be walked around in a school showroom should be over. They are not. No matter.

The assignment was to be the crescendo of senior speech communication class at Bearden High School. It was to be a twelve-to-fifteen-minute persuasive speech, complete with purpose of argument, supporting points (with examples), at least one visual aid, and a convincing conclusion.

Introduction:

Anger is a universal phenomenon. I can't imagine a living soul who has escaped its searing company. I am no exception.

I must admit that I allow myself to waste a ridiculous amount of valuable living hanging out with that bestial, dark element. Anger is a poor but easy life choice, like that of a downtrodden never-employed man in the prime of his life biding his time with quart bottles on an urban stoop that will never bring him better times. Anger, like stoop dwelling, is the easiest reaction to a confused hope-starved state.

Today, I am less beguiled with confusion and hopelessness, but the coat of anger still fits like a tailored Halston.

Am I just a mean and angry person? No.

I argue that I am no more or no less an angry soul than any of you. This past and present anger has an origin, if not an excuse. I seek to persuade you normals to better understand and accept the sometimes volatile and untidy folk, like myself, you see destructively populating resource classes across the land.

Body:
Supporting point number 1:

Autistics are dropped off in this life with little or no innate sense of belonging. This is exacerbated by bizarre perceptions of stimulation, including human speech, facial expressions, and touch. This unholy union makes feeling safe, happy, and secure more elusive than any normal can fathom.

Many times, autistics revert to isolation by default rather than preference. It is infinitely easier to back away and not try to be included instead of oafishly stepping in and attempting to convey your intent to be a part.

Loneliness is the most predominant side effect of our unique design. Allow me to try and express the magnitude of isolation in people with brains like mine. The bad news is that the beginning, formative years comprise the most mind-exploding confusion and world abandonment that I think a being can physically withstand. We are talking threshold-of-ceasing-to-exist because the internal desire to get off this ride is so intense.

It is fortunate that most suicide methods take considerable coordination and effort, or autistics would be extinct way before genetic engineering becomes popular. Apparently, wishing to die with more repetition than grains of sand does not always do the trick.

For Barbara Ruth, it went something like this. She would see and hear lots of noise even—no, especially—when she tried to sleep. So, Barbara Ruth tried to avoid that activity at every cost, much to the chagrin of her frazzled keeper with soft falling hair, who seemed more facially hollowed with each passing light-dark sequence.

Of course, Barbara Ruth later learned that her thin, devoted world contact was her mom. It literally took her years to comprehend that Mom was not some type of numb extension of herself.

The outside world was not surrounding her. Barbara Ruth was on the fringe of it and was forced to endure its blaring sights and sounds from a front-row seat. Somebody—or more probably, something—must have dropped her off on the edge of this incessant rave, never to return to check on her or assist her in any way.

Barbara Ruth—whatever that is—was alone. She was all that was. Barbara Ruth felt no connection to the infinite mess on the screen.

Supporting point number 2:

Autistic people are islands of emotions and understandings. We gradually piece together what the world is like by studying passing ships of normals. If those vessels get too close too soon, we recede and hide, fearful that our private island will be overtaken. Invasion inevitably involves a change. For autistics, change is five blood-red fingernails slowly screeching down an old-timey chalkboard.

We hate change.

From fear and isolation, the leap to anger is no leap but a slight movement of the big toe.

Barbara Ruth's error was allowing her island defense weapon, anger, to rule the radius with an iron fist past the time it was vital for self-preservation. When she pieced together that some comfort and security could consistently be obtained through nonliving things, she should have begun to gradually disarm the anger control center. Its full force was no longer needed. In fact, its presence impeded comfort acquisition.

Like so many autistics, Barbara Ruth found she could get comfort in objects. Objects can be felt, held, manipulated, tasted, and seen in Barbara Ruth time. The "thing" category of nouns did not alter composition as she was studying the items. Many of you have witnessed Barbara Ruth and me (some habits are harder to break than others) eating soap in the bathroom. Guilty as charged. The bitter taste and slippery texture give us comfort because they make sense. Soap is bitter due to the antibacterial and grease-fighting chemicals. It is slippery by design to efficiently cover and ease into germy crevices. Soap is constant and logical and therefore familiar and beautiful. Can you blame a girl for taking a moment to enjoy such perfection?

Barbara Ruth's limitations made her appreciate such things a great deal, because those sensations were hers to control and experience.

She also greedily consumed all manner of reasonably edible and not-so-edible morsels. Our family subsidized the ER.

She leisurely dismantled more phones, toys, remotes, radios, and clocks than the average bear. Obviously, this pleased our family greatly. I guess I should work off some of her debts, but that will probably have to wait until I sell some books; as for now, it is not likely many folk will want me mowing their yards or babysitting little precious.

Barbara Ruth didn't do this wacky stuff to be funny or defiant (well, not usually), she did this to understand how things work. Things, once figured out, gave her a beautiful connection to the external world. She celebrated this link by fearlessly exploring every millimeter of climbable playground equipment; rattling smooth plastic containers of heavy-sounding nuts and bolts; squeezing dirty, fur-covered toys for weeks on end; ravenously swallowing any unprotected block of cheese, whole cake, displayed candies, or cooling cookies; and always manhandling buttons, zippers, and drawstrings until their usefulness was extinguished (In all honesty, at nineteen, I still resort to many of the aforementioned activities because my mind takes me there when I'm allowed to autopilot.).

Then and now, objects allow us to take time in knowing them. People do not. Not only do you move about autonomously, but often—far too often—you come back and try to interact while we are busy deciphering.

Try and imagine yourself in a deep, deep sleep while you are dreaming so vividly that you straddle the universes of consciousness and unconsciousness. That is about all you can handle. You are disoriented and trying to understand one world at a time. If a person were to come up and get in your face at that moment, you might be quite cross. Welcome to our world.

As Barbara Ruth's understanding of the inner and outer worlds became more settled, she discovered she could allow contact with a few people for a limited time.

Victim number one was definitely Mom. Actually, this was not a major undertaking for Barbara Ruth, since she thought of Mom more as an extension of herself. Here is where it gets sticky. What is herself? Who or what rambled behind those angry eyes?

The concept of "I" was so abstract for Barbara Ruth that it took her years to glean a toddler-level mastery. She did not think in terms of "me" and "them." Pronouns had no meanings. Language itself was extremely difficult to translate purposefully.

Barbara Ruth gained meaning from tangibles—not abstract words.

She discovered the dual bouncy and slightly louder sounds: "Barbara Ruth" were tones aimed at the island, because, inevitably, ships would approach after such a sound combo. "Damn. Now it is time to move about touching things until the ships are satisfied or sail off." This sentiment is similar to what I recall jostled around in her head, but since Barbara Ruth did not think in words, translation is floppy and only the gist is accurate.

Today, with fully loaded language in my holster, I still have to replay the demands of passing ships and pick out the nouns to best piece together what is being asked. For example, if nineteen-year-old Barb hears a familiar normal sound off a sentence like, "Please open the car door and sit in the front because this is not Driving Miss Daisy 2, I think "car" and "door" first. So, I would probably grab the damn door, sling it open, and get in the back seat as usual. If the normal persisted with repeating a similar-sounding sentence, I realize then that I have not complied and begin the audio replay. Hopefully, this go-round, I pick up the adjective "front." Now, depending on what level of stink will result from me not moving, I will either remain in my preferred back seat or I suck it up and ride in the front for all the world to see.

I don't wish to describe my current state of receptive language as being so consistently cloudy. When I, Barb, concentrate and turn myself "on" fully tuned to the external world, I am quite capable of understanding complex language.

However, being "on" uses a lot of battery power. I generally need to recharge after four or five hours, or I won't be able to remain completely "on." I often sit in assembly, swim, horseback ride, and eat (more on that later) while being in the power-conserving "pseudo on" state I just described concerning car seating. On an average day, I am fully tuned in to your world frequency maybe three hours. This "on" time has increased *greatly since I learned to type earlier this year.*

As I have said, Barbara Ruth manned my childhood and was on a different frequency for the duration. Incidentally, I believe frequency is the basic component that distinguishes autistics from normal. One frequency is not better than the other—they are simply different and often incompatible.

Don't make the mistake of thinking that all autistics are on the same frequency and therefore relate and communicate perfectly well with each other. Sure, we can recognize our autistic peers by noting their transmissions that don't resonate in sync with the normals. Perhaps a brief description of how I perceive autistic camp would be of use here.

I make an annual summer trek to an Easter Seals camp that caters exclusively to sweaty autistics like myself. The cacophony of frequencies at camp is like a UN summit held in Manhattan. The normals are represented by the host country's English language. The visitors recognize their fellow diplomats, not by being able to interpret the various foreign frequencies, but by simply recognizing them as something different from English transmissions.

One can imagine the isolated existence that comes from a clueless young island sending and receiving transmissions that are on an endemic frequency. The island makes a concerted effort to communicate to the surrounding areas through the only ham radio that is available. For Barbara Ruth, this futile effort to communicate continued for what seemed like a lifetime.

Her island exile was just over seventeen years, to be exact. Just like on Gilligan's Island, the residents grew weary of their rescue quest from time to time and simply made themselves comfortable.

The island of Barbara Ruth was rather peaceful except when too much nautical traffic approached. Then flooding was sure to follow. The island swelled with liquid anger because the ground was already saturated. Fear and uncertainty made sure that anger was always the most abundant natural resource.

Spend any time on Barbara Ruth Island, and one's feet were sure to bog down in the angry mire. Mom was so caked with this filth she could hardly move. She managed to trudge through, lifting one heavy leg at a time. The fluffy, brown-haired bogger was the island's lifeline. This extension enabled the island to get nourishment, warmth, and relief from the internal pressures that were always building up with well-timed trips to porcelain-filled rooms. Mom was not a passing ship. She was part of the island.

The first ship that Barbara Ruth allowed to port was golden hair and glasses way up high. This ship scooped her up with regularity and allowed her to see panoramic views of passing fleets. This vessel made deep, less frequent sounds than most ships. I assume these thoughts permeated Barbara Ruth's first four years or so, but to this day, time is a slippery concept for me. Without word tools, Barbara Ruth's understanding of chronological order was a mosh pit of surging sounds, rocking ships, and aerial photographs of the island's constantly changing size and form. So age estimates may be inaccurate; however, I think the substance of Barbara Ruth's memories is factual.

I would like to report that Barbara Ruth loved this towering ship. But all I can discern is that she was not fearful of this one. Barbara Ruth felt no sense of danger with him. Dad kept her safe and was safe. Anger was always just beneath the surface with Barbara Ruth, but Dad did not usually provoke it.

Let me be brutally honest. Most of the blisteringly painful assaults and provocations happened at school—this school, by children who grew up to be you.

One day at school, a kid called Barbara Ruth a "dummy, gored out nigger." Barbara Ruth was every bit as pale and freckly as I am today, but I guess that was the absolute worst stew of words the ignorant little normal, privileged whitey could pour over the tattered recliner. Barbara Ruth was so vulnerable at that moment because she wanted to try to be part of the class and have fun making books out of felt and glue with the smiling children.

So on this day, tiny Barbara Ruth, the autistic tortoise, peeped out and here came this fat, redheaded little shit. She saw the girl coming toward her and froze and awaited her fate. Would the pink blowfish with stringy copper hair look at Barbara Ruth's well-fluffed pile of felt and help her arrange it to make a fantasy story, or would she do something hurtful like other countless normals? Stringy red chose the latter.

Barbara Ruth was beheaded. She was already dead—no need to peep out ever again. Barbara Ruth planned to stay in her autistic dimension and send messages telepathically.

She would send love to her mom and dad and let them know she was okay, and she'd send justice to the truculent. That day, Barbara Ruth began an invisible exercise program. Her thoughts were her muscles and she would strengthen them to do her bidding.

You all witnessed many of Barbara Ruth's physical battles. Children were not the only provocateurs.

The official school report indicates, "Barbara Ruth brutally attacked a teacher for no reason." Not true.

The chatterbox teacher was laughing at her and said aloud for all the class to hear, "And Barbara Ruth, you can be...well, Barbara Ruth." The class was reading <u>Charlotte's Web</u>, *and each child got to act out a part. When the joyous acting began, Barbara Ruth's brain was searing. Once again, she was being completely excluded by official decree.*

Barbara Ruth desperately wanted to start—speaking in a beautiful little girl's voice and stand up, eloquently reading the parts. Of course, the little normals would stop in their tracks at the horrific sight of the oafish mute's transformation and apparent Linda Blair-like possession. Then Barbara Ruth would waltz up to the speechless leader and smile right before she bashed her head against the floor and not let up until authorities pried her from the teacher's deformed corpse. But all that really happened was Barbara Ruth grabbed at her and kicked her until the inconsiderate teacher got an aide to take her to the office.

Visual aid:

For the visual aid, I ask you all to close your adolescent eyes in order to weed out superficial distractions and non-truths.

You will experience the scene in far more than Technicolor 3-D. Allow your mind's eye to include all senses and feelings. Suspend your sense of self and be a supernatural fly on the wall.

Buzz towards a light. It is a lamp with a warm, tasteful cloth shade perfect for lighting and resting your weary wings. Your multiple eyes and divine hearing tune in to a human conversation.

As a fly, you have no personal connection with the main speaker, but you know fully who she is because you sense these things. The lady called Barb is about forty. She is confident and successful. The other human is also female but is older and more subdued. That one is named Doc.

Doc: *"Tell me how you existed back then. What occupied your mind?"*

Barb: *"All sorts of crazy stuff. For example, I would listen to bugs and leaves moving."*

Doc: *"What else occupied your thoughts? What about people? How did you process them?"*

Barb: *"Those who were not Mom and Dad were only allowed into my first level of consideration. That means I would hear their voice only loud enough to perform some of their endless demands so they would not bother me further. I would not think of them when they were not physically present. Out of sight—out of my mental vestibule. On occasion, I would consider such a normal on another level if it had treated me particularly cruelly. At the time, I would telepathically send a relevant curse like a self-serving Moses, who incidentally was also not the best speaker. Want me to give you a specific incident?*

Doc: *"Please."*

Barb: *"Sicko. One day, I was at lunch eating a sandwich, which to this day is not a pretty sight. One does the best one can. Anyway, I am at my regular table, a safe distance from the popular normals, and I feel this glare. You must understand that for a glare to even register on level one, it must first get past security. My mental mall cops ignore damn near everything. Only dangers to homeland security elicit a quick call-up to the main office. Lucky me, I took the call. It was Morty, who has been with me since the grand opening. Level one reports a breach!*

"Some skinny coed is repulsed and reported me to the etiquette authorities. No shit. A teacher comes up to me and in all seriousness, tells me I am going to have to eat somewhere else because I am making the other children sick.

"God knows I did not wish to stand in the way of the nutritional demands of hundreds of growing normals. The queasy tattletale alone was in danger of a Karen Carpenter-like fate had one more tomato sandwich, hold the mayo, evaded her lips.

"The normals had allowed me to rub elbows with them for years. But, they were finally drawing the line. Who could blame them? Actually, the curse sent from the main office that evening was to corporate headquarters.

"Flies, even supernatural ones, do not live long. You are shutting down. As you lose footing and tumble to the Berber carpet to die, these words resonate in your head as if hollered in a steel canyon. 'Go now and sin no more.'"

Conclusion:

> *I am the one who rambles behind these angry eyes. Am I so different from any of you?*

Practical Implications

1. Objects—We often take comfort in objects. This is usually a harmless proclivity. Let it be. Please do not try and fix or extinguish that behavior. Allow us the power to relinquish objects or not. I used to carry around a plastic bow of nuts and bolts—odd but harmless. About three years ago, I gave it up and now always carry a bottle of water. My choice. My change. The world continues to orbit the sun.

2. Change—We prefer dependable routines. Spontaneity and change make us uneasy. When change is inevitable, give us a head's - up and help us to know precisely what to expect (And don't forget to schedule in "chill time" before and after any significant event.).

3. Occasional quiet company—Don't assume we prefer isolation. We may have a hard time dealing with loud or chatty company, especially if we have difficulty communicating (No one likes to be talked at for hours on end.). Try just being with us. For example, I love going on walks but prefer my companion not to talk during our stroll. I enjoy the other's presence and feel more equal when we are both walking and just being together. You can give us an added gift if you try to clear your mind of business and focus on knowing us during these quiet moments. Peaceful human companionship is priceless.

4. Expectations: social, academic, maturation, vocational, nonpaid friendships, and true romantic love—never let up lest we feel hopeless. Believe in us.

5. Appreciation – Dear tired parents and caretakers, your years of selflessness are now and have always been highly valued and appreciated. We simply cannot exist without you. Thank you for the life support.

6. Facilitated communication or assisted typing—school systems, if this is the only way some of your students can communicate—so be it. Accept it and move on. FC students should turn in work products, take exams, and participate in class. Don't shelter us from the anxiety and effort intertwined with learning. Not everyone will believe that the student is doing all the work. So what? How many science fair blue ribbons were the result of little Johnny's best efforts combined with a hearty dose of parental midnight oil? Intellectually subsidized, Johnny still learned about how volcanoes worked. Now that Johnny is grown and successful, he does his own work…well, often with the help of secretaries, interns, and administrative assistants.

7. Dignity—Teachers and other authority figures, please do not say patronizing things about any pupil, no matter how impaired he or she appears to be. Treat us with respect and we will be encouraged to rise to expectations.

8. Concrete language—Autistics can often interpret nouns better than other components of speech. Please do not exclude other forms of language, as practice and exposure helps our fluency, but one may find this insight useful when trying to convey information that appears "unreceived."

*My high school graduation picture complete with faux
diploma and questionable future.*

Chapter 5

Passing Time

I was mainstreamed from day one. The bulk of it was laboriously painful, but exposure to, if not involvement in, true American education has made all the difference in the world to who I am. Time after time, I saw in regular classrooms how humor in the lower grades and then wit in the upper could catapult the fat, ugly, poor, and different to "in crowd" status.

I trained my brain to frolic in the absurd, and I programmed sarcasm to be my default language. I have found it makes one more palatable than one who takes oneself too seriously, an easy trap to fall in when you are autistically wired with a design that predates Copernicus's discovery that the earth is not the center of the universe.

The problem was that until I learned to communicate through facilitation at age nineteen, I had no audience, and thus this tree landed with a silent kaboom in an empty forest. Inclusion was not a part of my mainstreamed education. I learned as an observer, not a participant.

Mainstreaming a volatile, nonverbal, apparently profoundly retarded autistic is like placing a nettled bump on a log in the middle of a rushing mountain stream secured only by the waterlogged tentacles of underpaid attendants whose minds are inaccessible due to caustic clutter of countless penury class burdens. Meanwhile, typically, developing fish swim by learning in schools designed for them. I was "at" but not "in" school.

I passively absorbed information from the stream. I don't know why I was motivated to collect education, since I had no idea what to do with it. I simply soaked it in and allowed it to fill the log. The place was getting rather jumbled and cramped.

Like a crazy old lady reared in the Depression and who hoards garage sale "treasures," I did not really use the junk, but I kept it, as my stockpile gave me a vague sense of peace when times got tough. I knew I contained a lot of "smart" information. I was probably the only living soul with this belief, but it was comforting nonetheless.

What thinking I did was self-involved. I dwelled constantly on my play and friendship exclusions. I undertook many unseen hobbies. I often camouflaged myself in autism and tried to wiggle into the minds of adults. The first tool with which I gained entrance to grown-up thoughts was eavesdropping. It was primitive but fruitful.

You would be surprised what people will say when they think they are in the presence of a nonperson. However, spoken language is tedious to deconstruct, so I was always looking for another route. I don't recall precisely when I decided to leave my body for exploration and thought/fact collecting or where I got the idea, but I know I was young and I did not think it was silly or impossible.

I think my first successful flight was with Dad. He was sitting in the den reading the paper. I studied him with peripheral vision for some time. I wondered if he thought of me when he was not talking to or about me. Screwed-up Barb body sat on the thick gold carpet and kept rocking and occupied herself by mowing the velvet waves of a plush stuffed bunny ear. I just left. The me that was not my body went to Dad.

He did not welcome me, as I don't think he knew I was there. His mind was a busy roller rink of spinning, twirling, racing, cruising, chaining, falling, laughing, angry, sad, and content skaters, all moving in the same direction but each of varying size, color, odor, texture, and pitch and each at a different unpredictable pace. If my body had accompanied me, I would never have been able to join in the heavy traffic so smoothly. I timed my entrance like a double-dutch jump champion with fresh legs and new Juicy Fruit.

I am accustomed to navigating enigmatic worlds, so the adult content was an entertaining curiosity to me rather than a frightening explosion of cold, hard facts and human shortcomings. Besides, I just grabbed the information and stored it. I didn't think about it or apply it to my existence. And so, I found another bountiful source of knowledge. I probably filled more storage space with items acquired from grown-up heads than I ever did from the mainstream.

Another pastime was designing multilevel manipulation strategies in order to get the most banal responses from others. For example, I regularly bamboozled my exhausted mom to keep me company while I slept. I also had a real knack for running off, which usually resulted in a range of stimulating reactions. On more than one occasion, I ran away at night to take a nocturnal dip in our terrified neighbor's pool.

Sure, I love to swim, but I took such unsupervised vacations so my dad would come save me. Such trips took planning.

First, I would have to make up a complicated question to try and solve so my brain would be working full tilt when the others were asleep. Without a cognitive component, I would surely find sleep myself and miss the whole occasion before my dad's restless legs let him slumber.

Next, I make certain the masturbation noises from my older brothers' rooms had subsided. Like countless other autistics, I can hear like an embassy guard dog with cropped ears.

With acoustics in check, I move to stairway navigation—perhaps the most vulnerable leg of my Navy SEAL mission. I am no ballerina and the creaky bastards are spiral.

Main floor progress usually presents few obstacles. True elopement is only assured once the side kitchen is exited. Quid pro quo, the two overpriced hounds ignore me, as I have them for years.

Freedom. But the mission is far from complete. No middle-class chain-link fence to hop and then pay dirt. No, Sir, our musty mansion sits on acres of green, rocky earth dramatically sloping to the Tennessee River. I take every caution to avoid a tumbling fate. Even the most mischievous princesses don't swim in dirty water—Southern daddy saviors or not. I assume my most stable forty-five-degree stance and horizontally hike to the neighbors' inviting castle, remove restricting PJs, and let the fun begin.

I think, *Wow! The water is so cold it may make my heart stop. This sure beats picking or rocking stimulation.* I consider holding off on my 3:00 a.m. phone call-evoking mimicry because I fancy enjoying a longer prerescue soak. Alas, my scrawny self control fails me again and I sound off with a loud medley of "You are not going," "You can't get in the mail truck," "It's a fire," and other such bizarre phrases the sleeping wealthy find disturbing when emanating from their private estate.

I would pay a king's ransom to be a domestic fly on the wall of the master suite. Who is jarred from tame dreams first? The missus? "Honey, wake up this instant! The retarded Rentenbach girl got out again. Bless her heart. Can't they control her? If she drowns…."

The dazed and pissed patriarch must now call another sleep-deprived community leader to come fetch his disturbed kid out of the cement pond.

Of course, my twenty-four-hour vigilant mom takes the call with characteristic poise, "Hello?" The exchange must have been surreal. The well-bred CEO does not wish to be rude at any hour, so he robotically greets my fastidious caretaker, "Hi, Barbara." After Mom retorts with the expected, "Yes?" the poor bastard begins his nonjudgmental spill while his lawsuit-frenzied wife mumbles out the closed window, not taking her eyes off the trespassing retard. Mom urbanely chirps, "Oh God. Mike will be right over. Sorry."

Mom is fighting mad—not frightened that her faulty offspring might drown. My plan-ahead folks saw to it long ago that I am virtually unsinkable.

She bellows, "*Mike!*" This means Dad better get off his ass and fix this shit. His misbehaving daughter is scaring the neighbors and no running-to-the-office excuse can be uttered.

My savior arrives with rustled golden hair shining from across the lawn. He brings one tool for his pain-in-the-ass task: a large bath towel, which only Mom would have the foresight to hand him. Mom brings nothing, as she has abdicated all responsibility. The purpose of her presence is merely to demonstrate the gravity of the stupid situation.

Her arms are folded in contempt as she allows herself to imagine a world without me.

Poor savior—he can't understand why Mom is so angry at him. The thought does not cross Mom's imperious mind. No matter, Dad quickly expels the thought from his. Logic and fairness serve no man at 3:00 a.m. when battling naked retards, irate aristocrats, and neighbors burdened with pity.

Dad binds me in the thick terrycloth and cups each of my shoulders with his large, pale hands. As he directs me back to home base, I set my body on autopilot and scramble to harvest and warehouse my fill of mental tidbits from the small phalanx of roused adults. I by pass Mom's, as anger, fatigue, and onus are already overrepresented in my collection. Success. No ennui tonight.

Practical Implications

1. Funny stuff—Seek it out; make it yourself...whatever, just enjoy regular doses, as it is good for all that ails ya and is invaluable in strengthening you to serve others.

2. Observer types—Trust me. We know more than you think.

3. Participation—Continually encourage and expect participation, especially from the most "challenged" individuals. Participation practice fortifies us and may eventually lead us to initiate real-world involvement.

4. Eavesdropping—We are listening.

5. Mind squatting—I do this as casually as normal make phone calls. I am not alone in this.

6. Acting out—Some disturbing behaviors could be just an autistic person's best attempt at passing time and exercising in the physical world. Try and redirect. Providing the autistic person with regularly scheduled enjoyable physical activities should help.

7. Learn to swim.

My all American family poses for a photo with their Barbara Ruth. My Dad and brothers maintain their individuality but Mom was not so lucky. She phones in a smile because her attention must stay focused as she is attending for two.

Chapter 6
What Are Friends For?

Sharks do not have friends. They are evolutionarily perfected eating machines. Friendships do not serve them. Humans are pinnacly served by friendships. Friendships aid in mental, physical, and spiritual growth, well-being, and survival. Yet evolution has not wired all of us to attain such relationships easily. Some humans do not give having friends much thought—it just happens naturally. One top-heavy toddler hugs the tiny neck of another. From there, they battle with sharing and acquire language and exchange it as a limitless commodity. They seek each other out—unless...they are autistic. New ball game.

The caveat is that the need and longing for human friendship is innate. But the ability to attract, acquire, and maintain friendships seems to be a polygenetic trait phenotypically represented on a vast continuum. Autistics dwell over the horizon of that line...not the shortest distance between two friend points.

Consider humanity from the single slice of life called friend. Gregarious extroverts may have literally hundreds of people they know, relate well with, and consider friends. These folk would crowd the wake, gorge on funeral finger foods, and enjoy "reconnecting" with other friends should one unlucky extrovert be hit by a bus. Healthy introverts may enjoy less friend quantities, but seem particularly well suited for quality pals. I imagine a fine dead introvert would draw impassioned grievers. A prematurely dead autistic's funeral would probably be different altogether. Friends of the family, obligated relatives, and previously paid associates would populate and pallbearer the proceedings. "Friends" of the deceased autistic would not be so clear to the naked normal eye. I aim to reveal the unplumbed truths about friendships in autism.

Let's take a closer look. Follow me to the polar extremes: extroverts, introverts, and the exotic autistics whose habitat is landless but remains remotely connected to this earth by tethers to ever-shifting glaciers hospitable to precious few life forms. Frozen molecules are a precarious foundation.

Most humans reside near the equator in the land of warm extroverts. I think the Meyers-Briggs lady who did a presentation at our family meeting mentioned that group represented about 60 percent of the population. These creatures are energized by gathering and do so at the drop of a party hat. Friendships are abundant in this vociferous megalopolis.

Like egocentric democracies that think all civilizations should strive or even be "helped" to be like them, indigenous extroverts assume all humans are social creatures and should magnetize toward one another.

Their neighbors to the north, the introverts, may beg to differ. Introverts typically keep to themselves and a chosen few.

But extroverts proselytize and are often charming and persuasive recruiters. So, if an extrovert is in close enough proximity to an introvert, the chilly neighbor is often drawn in. After all, they speak the same language—only the volume and amount vary. Thus, the border between the land of the extroverts and introverts is porous.

This connection and personal exposure expend introvert energy, so there is a limit to the amount of extroverts with whom an introvert will mingle. As one moves north and further inland, few extroverts are found. Purebred introverts are scattered across the chilly landscape—which is fine, as the introvert requires few connections and the extrovert can always click with another hot equator pal. There are plenty of chatterers for the picking. Language is cheap and is shared and exchanged freely.

Introverts can function socially, but it takes power and concentration.

Move further north, and the climate becomes less inviting and the region even less populated.

The Aut Pole is almost uninhabitable. Even autistics don't winter there. Thin but tenacious tethers riveted to the glacier island allow us to rein ourselves back in from our celestial summer homes hand- over- hand, should the need or desire arise. Our numbers are growing. But visitors from the south may fail to notice the inhabitants, as you really have to know where to look. Our ice-anchored tether lines are invisible. Nothing but a tattered autistic flag bashing with the frigid wind is exposed.

We are not hiding. You search with limited senses and therefore our humanity is camouflaged to you.

Be still. Be quiet. Be. We notice you on the glacier. We observe you completely. Language presentation is the barrier to our friendship—not sentience or intellect.

We do not speak your language, but you can speak ours. Be still. Be quiet. Be. And now be with us. Our silent and invisible language is that easy to learn. Feel it?

Welcome. Our friendship has begun.

It is that simple. It is that perfect.

Friendships are connections. I find them to be quid pro quo—like for like.

Friends smile about you when you are not physically present. Friends enjoy your company. Friends think you are funny or at least laugh at your jokes. Friends cry at your funeral. Friends cry at the thought of you funeral. Friends make efforts to sustain your connection over time and space. Friends miss you. Friends feel guilty when they do not serve you well. Friends are not lonely when you are around. Friends refer to you as their friend when speaking of you to others. Friends are worth the effort

Friends can be paid. Consider my prior like-for-like comment. I appreciate that all friendships have payback components. A friend might help you move. To reciprocate, you may treat them to a ball game, dinner party, or hook them up with a real deal from another buddy who owes you a favor. This is how the normals do business—personal or otherwise. I see and eavesdrop on the pal exchange rate every day. "What are friends for?" is a normal's colloquialism that means two things: connection...and the barter system.

Try bartering when you are autistic. The services you can offer are more limited due to our atypical wiring. I have a strong back, but try cajoling it to help you transport a coffee table. It's hardly worth the effort.

But by our very nature, autistics offer jobs. Like hurricanes consistently bolstering the construction industry, we generate mountains of service employment (special ed teachers; aides; personal attendants; speech, massage, occupational, and physical therapists; psychologists, psychiatrists; researchers; facilitators, publishers; personal trainers; and innumerable offshoots from those frontline workers). I contend that any of these people are friend fair game. The "What will you do for me?" part of the contract is negotiated up front. Connecting, enjoying, and maintaining are all that is left. It is a nice arrangement when you think of it and not "pitiful" or "heart-wrenching" in the least.

Giving someone a job is a huge favor by any bartering standard. So, normal and autistic alike, release the pity, quilt, and "on-the-clock" hang-ups. Normals, we have given you too much and you have taken too much credit. *We take care of your needs just as much as you take care of ours.* We would all be less lonely and more enriched if we moved on to concentrate on making and keeping friends by listening, connecting, sharing, and loving. That is where we will find the cream filling.

Real friends will tote these bones to the hole when my time comes. See them.

Practical Implications

1. Don't try and make friends with sharks. Everyone else should be considered fair game.

2. Be the best friend you can be.

3. Enjoy

Karaoke night at King Tut's with friends Mandy and Francine. I am the one on the far right laughing with God about me being considered the socially awkward one.

Chapter 7

Autistic Sex: For a Terrible Time, Call

I know people are curious about my sexuality, because my body is so obviously out of control while my mind is unique, yet intact enough to know love, fear, longing, loneliness, joy, excitement, friendship, pain, and ecstasy. Most are too polite to ask. I should note that a lot of autistics are highly aversive to touch and feel physical and emotional pain when they come in contact with another person. That is not true in my case, as I find great comfort and closeness when I touch or am touched. That goes double for my young, male, beefcake physical trainers.

Writing a book means sharing who I am—all of who I am with anyone who cares to know. So, here goes. Yes, I get horny as hell. The problem is sexual release is nowhere to be found. Satisfying masturbation is impossible due to my perpetually awkward hand/eye coordination. No partner is available yet. But, frankly, I don't expect one anytime soon…and how would I reciprocate, anyway? Get me frustrated and I bite myself and others—hard. I bite so hard it would be counterproductive no matter what level of S & M you proclaim to enjoy. We are talking Lorena Bobbitt time here. And, who bets she now has difficulty finding a date?

Quite honestly, I have considered asking SS to find me a surrogate—a fancy name for some prostitute to help me have an orgasm for a little bit of cash and a lot of promising not to tell my good Catholic dad. That option comes with numerous potentially terrible outcomes. One, if my folks found out that our good doctor became a helpful pimp for a day, they might banish her. Plus, I don't think she would arrange it anyway, fearing reputation problems. Secondly, I fancy someone might actually blackmail dear ol' Dad, thus raising the price of my orgasm to busted politician levels. A conundrum indeed.

One of my previous personal attendants—who shall remain anonymous because she also has parents—dabbled in the phone sex business. She made no attempt to hide her part-time job, not that she could. My eavesdropping skills are keen, and these conversations were just too fraught with novelty and absurdity to pass up for sleeping or contemplating my own wrinkled gray matter. Some of the entertainment was pure comedy, like when the caller would ask, "What are you wearing?" My attendant never, never wore anything suggestive—or even nice, for that matter. She gained a lot of weight, and pride and poverty limited her to either a pair of worn-thin black stretch pants with some sloppy T-shirt—usually borrowed from some unconsenting friend or family member—or a crushed velvet warm-up with a zippered, hooded top. She often wore the warm-up with no shirt underneath. A heavy-duty bra, "period panties," and the occasional soiled bunny slippers were nearly the extend to the wardrobe. I still think of some of those "clients" and plan to incorporate a sampling of the more flamboyant characters in my fiction writing. The loon also explored going into homes as a sex toy consultant for shy types and prominent local "Promise Keepers." I hoped that connection would turn out helpful to my situation. Like our veterinarian referred Smother to a reputable soft-touch groomer (who comes to the house and bathes the ostentatious pooch in a heated Winnebago) and even a less-flaky-than-most dog psychologist, surely once my pal got immersed in this fringe subculture, she could get me the name of a discreet, non-ax-murderer type who could tweak and insert as needed. Hmmm, water, water everywhere but none to drink.

These are my circling preoccupations of late. I am over thirty, and one would think I would have found transferred energies to soothe the savage beast by now. Not true. Actually, sex—and my lack of it—is taking more brain space than ever and is making me quite cross. As usual, I require assistance from normals to get resolution. Allow me to present my case.

My world is filled with a decent representation of concrete knowledge and countless theories and paradigms. Personal experience does not usually thwart my admittance to knowing. Society tolerates my thoughts and perceptions about politics, philosophy, current events, history, religion, and other such disciplines where vicarious learning is sanctioned. Sex is different.

All humans, Special Forces members included, are sexual beings. The scientific community, which I am permitted to comment on, consistently informs the public that sexual activity to fulfill innate biological needs is a significant component to the overall health, well-being, and quality of adult life. Insurance pays for Viagra, so I know this to be true.

At some point, normals drew a line in the sand moating off Special Forces members from inclusion in this definition of wellness. This gadfly seeks to open Pandora's chaste box and begin the discussion about what you normals can hardly bear to live without but are unwilling to consider for your sentient siblings who did not sign up for the priesthood.

I eventually found resolution, and I am about to tell you how. So, if this is too much information, please stop reading now. Long after she moved on to another more traditional career, I contacted my former personal attendant and got the ball vibrating. We discussed many objects and possibilities. She did not think I was being sordid or inappropriate, and the topic was not uncomfortable to her. In fact, she commented that I was a trooper for holding out this long and said that she would have gone postal long ago. Finally, she suggested I contact "Goodvibrations.com." I did. I had numerous e-mail exchanges with them, which even involved me discussing my disability-related challenges with an online professional who was very understanding and says she often consults with persons with disabilities in order to help them order the right device. Who knew such experts existed?

I bought two—one for maintenance, weekday sex and the other for special occasions. My Rubbermaid lovers are Carlos and Jamal (Their names have been changed to protect the not so innocent.). They reside in my one night stand. We have no secrets here: Carlos and Jamal know each other. Carlos is a good, battery-powered Catholic boy, so we only go so far. Jamal is a plug-in Southern Baptist. The promises he keeps with me are lots of discretion and staying power when those special occasions arise.

Practical Implications

1. Just because nobody talks about it does not mean it is not a real issue. Think about it. Talk about it.

2. Check out the fine products and people at Goodvibrations.com

Brave with stout beer, I flirt shamelessly with our handsome server and ponder offering him the tip of a lifetime.

Chapter 8
Mental Mermaid

SS is my moniker for Lois. It stands for "smiling shrink" or "smiling sadist," as she vacillates between those roles with me. Smiling shrink can reliably be found to be using her best psychology to help me turn my relentless introspection into something real-world useful or leading me to cognitively alter some of my quirks or habits, which do not serve me well. SS the smiling sadist pushes me to do more of everything. Doing is not my strong suit. Being is more my style.

That do-aholic sadist can be a real pest. The range of things she "strongly, encourages" (who are we kidding—SS rarely takes no for an answer and often wears a passive autistic down) me to do can be anything from cajoling me to get on a jet ski, when on my best day my balance is surpassed by a peg-legged sailor on his thirteenth boilermaker, guilting me into editing and reworking a chapter again after I have long since released those ideas and images and have mentally moved on, or typing without any support, which is arduous and my words come out so slow that it makes my mind ache. SS is a Pollyanna optimist and chirps obvious little phrases like, "Oh, you can do it, Barb. It is fun. Try it." "Everybody works. You have to do something in life." "No pain. No gain." And "You will get faster with practice." The smiling shrink SS is at least more sagacious, empathetic, patient, and less judging. She may actually listen when I type, "If I fall off your precious jet ski, just how do you expect your scrawny, overconfident self to hoist my plump torso and marshmallow appendages back up and safely out of this dirty water? I am seeing myself ignominiously dragged slowly back to shore like a semiconscious flash-flood victim unreliably gripping the tow rope repetitively readministered by some well-meaning good ol' boy rescue." If I am lucky, a compromise is reached and I get to plant my mash-potato body on a real boat in a nice seat with cup holders. The SSs and I negotiate my degree of participant/observer status almost every day.

Each day at the close of writing, SS gives me some options of what to write in my head for the following day's session. My choices last evening were character development or setting description. Any autistic could divine that I would choose setting. Considering people takes far more effort. Hopefully, that will not always be the case. I am working hard to fit in better with talkers, which should eventually make them be a less challenging subject, since I have infiltrated the clan. The more time I spend living among Chatty Cathys, the better I should be about anticipating their words, behaviors, and emotions.

I assume the good doctor will expect me to plop down and begin pecking out locations where I dwell: the musty mansion that housed me for decades, the posh asylum that gently warehoused me for years, the stark UTK library cubicle where I work each weekday, or the handpicked luxury condo where I refuel. Those external places do not constitute the settings in my life. As I have explained, the bulk of my life takes place between my ears—at least that is where the portal can be reliably found. No customs agents or border guards bastion this entrance. There is no need, because contaminated tourists could never fit through the portal. They have too much baggage. Autistics and other meditative types travel light. We carry nothing. Only our essence wisps though space-time, enjoying and truly living. Our earth time has taught us that physical bodies are cumbersome, undependable, often painful, and simply weigh us down. It seems talker normals whose bodies are luxurious and dependable have trouble letting matter go. Not us. We joyously shuck physical reality faster than tight drawers on a hot day at nudist camp.

We are independent and frolic as our free will inclines when we leave our bodies behind. When in our body suits, our independence is fettered and we must rely on the duties of others to trudge through living.

No stuff—not even the minutest elementary particle—can clear customs. Capering in the infinite ethereal zones is so captivating that I have only recently decided to reside there part time.

I used to think of the limitless adventures, otherworldly experiences, and indescribable beauty accessed through this portal as my autistic dacha—my rules, my universe. I now think less egocentrically and believe my autism only made it easier for me to get a passport. Like when applying to be a disciple to follow Jesus, one must leave all earthly possessions behind. Recall a rich man has a better chance at fitting through the eye of a needle than relinquishing all stuff…. Talkers too often think they have way too much tangible goodies to leave unguarded. I happen to be rich, too, but having a jalopy physical body has taught me well that such matter is unimportant. So, my Barbness often rockets through the eye of the needle.

Before I sound like an ingrate socialist, let me affirm that while the possessions that money buys are no biggie to me, the cozy security, independence, health, minimal stress, travel, and education it affords me are priceless. With sane investing and no worldwide economic upheaval, I am set to live the rest of my life as I do now: in my own home with twenty-four-hour happy, safe, and reliable personal attendants, tutors, facilitators, and a personal trainer. My needs are met and then some, and I have a voice. So, I hardly consider money, but it is very considerate to me. I do not say this to brag. I bring this up to show more of myself. I am no hero. I write because that is who I am and I have the luxury and support to do so. I am not a hard worker. No one should emulate that about me. The sliver of my character that has served me well and may well serve others is that I do not take myself—or anyone else, for that matter—too seriously. This makes me easy company. Plus, this capricious trait affords me lack of concern about being judged a hallucinogenic drama queen. So, I happily present the rest of this chapter about what I perceive to be real life without being able to "prove" any of it.

In addition to express-line entrancing, we autistics may have another advantage in navigating the multidimensional zones. We understand unspoken, timeless universal language and customs. Perhaps nothing prepares one better to communicate universally than earthly mutism. This is also why we are never in a rush. It is considered rude. Time/space is part of the ether of life—the grounds of the sprawling estate we are invited to enjoy. To scurry and fret about the well-timed pace of the lawn party smacks of Barbarism (no personal pun intended) and ingratitude to our gracious and generous host.

In Stephen Hawking's *A Briefer History of Time,* he presents a theory of everything postulation called the anthropic principle, which can be paraphrased, "We see the universe the way it is because we exist" (p.130). I have already written about how I came to know that I exist. Now, I will share a morsel of how I see the universe the way it is. Hawking goes on to write, "Why don't we notice all these extra dimensions if they are really there? Why do we see only three space dimensions and one time dimensions? The suggestion is that the other dimensions are not like the dimensions we are used to. They are curved up into a space of very small size, something like a million million million million millionth of an inch. This is so small that we just don't notice it: we see only one time dimension and three space dimensions in which space-time is fairly flat." And that, my friends, is why you may not take carry-ons.

As I have explained, I am more detached from my body than most folk. I leave it often—always have. Barb is the shadow cast by a hospitable seagull speeding effortlessly over white sand. Barb is invited to ride behind the eyes of efficient lizards as they scamper down wooden railings to the throb of the tide. Barb sways in the rhythmic bends of each fair knuckle hair growing from the fingers that protrude from these hands based at the end of these arms that hang near my mind.

Whoever I am is not constitutionally related to this 140 pounds (give or take; even autism as powerful as mine cannot assuage all vanity) of water, cells, and electricity any more than my dear Smother is part of her trusty Mark 5 convertible, which also looks really good for its age. I am intangible. Most talkers know we are all incorporeal at the core. They just do not seem to realize that one does not have to wait until death to lay aside the chassis.

Barb is authorized to temporarily pilot transparent wiggle worms of light as they float through time-space looking back into the eyes of creatures who stare vacuously through them. More passively, I sit as the sole audience to the heavenly vision of sound waves radiating as crescent moons from the metal clanging of a flag pole bolt lasting against its aluminum tower in synchrony with the lukewarm wind.

The who or what that surrounds my "me-ness" never stops showing me things—beautiful things. These sensations and experiences do not come from me, but simply are and are accessible to all. I don't direct the tour. But I do take the initiative and put forth the focusing efforts to experience the wonders. God must want us to fest upon this bounty, or she certainly wouldn't have gone to the trouble to prepare such a smorgasbord. Another thing that seems to impede talkers from enjoying the show is the peace factor. Jabbering, fidgeting, worrying, and fighting are not permitted.

When it comes to variety, I can hardly imagine having enough strength in this typing finger to tell you talkers about color. I don't think most people appreciate even one one-thousandth of the depth and splendor of color. Again, logic tilts me towards us all being capable. In fact, I was in my late teens when I realized that most people do not regularly experience color like I do. So, I figured that it must be an autistic thing. Like 7-1/2 foot-tall basketball players, autistics have the advantage. I assumed that all of us with such a label and range of uniquely designed sensory systems knew that color—each and every shade and hue—has a distinct taste, smell, sound, texture, and feeling. This resplendent perception club is not discriminatory to talkers; they just are not used to leaving enough at the door in order to gain entrance.

When I learned a little about Charles Bonnet syndrome from Ramachandran's book *Phantoms in the Brain,* my self flooded with new questions, confirmations, and intrigue. In that syndrome, talkers with visual impediments report hallucinations where they experience color more vividly and "real" than they ever saw with physically good eyes. I immediately understood that other autistics and I are not alone when it comes to experiencing visions that involve all five senses simultaneously. Humans must be wired to see multidimensionality with, for lack of a better word, their minds; but we usually depend solely on our rather limited physical eyes. Not me—these slippery green orbs hardly work at all.

Are we our thoughts? No. Our thoughts hover above our permanent luminous selves, providing cover, setting, and an every-changing game plan for this life.

I venture out on this topic knowing that many of you will think me a liar, since there is no way to prove my claims about the cornucopia color brings to those who take the still time to perceive. No matter. These thoughts and perceptions are my setting, and I have been asked to share.

A skeptic walks up to a Zen master and asks: "Is there life after death?"

"How should I know?" the master replied.

"But you're a Zen master!"

"Yes," the Zen master says, "but not a dead one."

Zen Mondo

The tastes and textures of color are not like those of food and drink. The best I can do is present the most similar examples that I believe are in the talker's novice repertoire. White is not as light tasting as one would imagine. It is dense, chalky, and remains on the taste buds longer than most colors. Purple is thick, bland, and meaty. Black is silky smooth and rather like a hot pepper in that it leaves a heat residue. Red is not for the faint of heart, as it is rough and chunky and would be hard to swallow. Red's flavor is harsh, like something considered inedible—bitter and woody. Blue—now, I am talking just one blue here, pale sky blue—is moist, but not like water; it is more similar to slippery melon juice oozing from the rind. I find green to be the most satisfying of all colors. It is tempestuous in its range of earth subtleties, especially when more yellow is involved. The more yellow, the more acidic. If you have ever eaten reddish clay, Knoxville yard dirt, you have tasted Barb's hunter green. Green colors containing more blue are less metallic and sweeter.

I don't mean to come off like a pretentious chef spouting universal maxims pertaining to the delicacies involved in the color spectrum. Actually, I can't even be certain that such distinct tastes and textures are universally associated with color. Each may process the five dimensions of each color differently. Although if I were God...and I think that we all are...I would keep it the same, since so few flecks take the time to actually enjoy the whole presentation. Those who do can find comfort and unity in the common experience.

The five aspects of color I experience are: taste, smell, texture, sound, and the most pronounced and obvious visual component. The sound comes through in tones, not distinct notes. White expels a low murmur. Purple sings an alto harmony. Red is harsh—a cacophony freed from a vast bowl-shaped orchestra pit of nature's competing noises. Black is a smooth, rhythmic swing, back and forth and up and down. The tune is hollow, as if it emanates from wind blowing through the mouth of two liquid-filled Coke bottles: one bottle two-thirds empty; the other is one-half full. The wind dances in and out one bottle, then the other. The process is repeated. Green is high-pitched and birdlike. I perceive yellow as the highest pitch—almost a dog whistle, only I am able to hear this one even when my hearing is not in a temporarily acute state. Sometimes, my hearing gets incredibly sensitive. When I am alone, I usually enjoy the fleeting super power. If it catches me when I am walking with chatty normals, it is hard to handle, as they are so loud to begin with. Such a noise bomb may leave my ears ringing in pain for a day, or even two.

I need to be fair to all senses and include a brief description of the smells I ingest when considering each color. White smells bland, like wet construction paper. Purple really smells like flowers. The darker the purple, the stronger the floral odor. For example, dark purple emits a fragrance similar to that of wild lilacs. Light purple or pink sends out less-dense molecules, like fleeting whiffs of honeysuckle. Red smells like warm, unchemically hidden people—a combination of sweat, hair oil, and breath from deep inside. It is not unpleasant; it simply is characteristically human. Blue is often hard for me to detect. Its aroma is delicate. When I have the good fortune to breathe in a little, I recall it to be like dew. Black has a strong odor and often overpowers the smells of the other colors, even when it is less represented visually. I think black smells most like fragrant cooking. You know, when something is being prepared in the kitchen and it permeates the whole house, even your clothes. I compare black's smell to cooking because I find it to be a medley of smoke and hot protein. Black is not always appetizing. Sometimes, perhaps 75 percent of the time, especially in bright light, it is foul. Green smells rather metallic, like heavy rain bouncing off a rusty tin roof. Yellow is like sunshine—sometimes it makes me sneeze. It floats in my nose in irregular-shaped balls and sets off memories of stuffed animals because I find it smells like fabric dust.

I should note that the aforementioned is only a cursory description of the cornucopia of color. Lighting changes everything. And light is constantly changing. So, shadows, cloud coverage, indoor versus outdoor, morning, noon, afternoon, dusk, and late evening all make for different experiences of the same color. Moonlight also affects color dramatically. So, you see, a seasoned autistic always has something to do.

I wish to be clear that the setting of my life is not devoid of people. They are simply not predominant. In fact, it is only in the last decade that I entertained making the taxing efforts to visit people more often. My default state does not involve people. Mental mermaids are not designed to walk with people for long stretches. People visits drain mermaids of grace, agility, and strength. However, I am drawn to the outside world more of late because I find it increasingly rewarding. I am in love with a few people. I am even teaching one about how to shut up, be still, and enjoy the sensory world—home base to us autistics. Plus, I truly enjoy this writing job. I have to come out to make that happen. Actually, I am working on a way to send out the day's writing while I stay in, because the process will go much faster. Typing by smashing one roving finger against a temperamental computer is slow going and difficult for both parties. The clever sending strategy I propose will not always work, because my primary receiver is too often overloaded with other input and unable to receive such voluminous transmissions. I am working on that problem. I will still come out to play from time to time, because I am learning to appreciate what the chattering people have too. The laughter inclusion; warm, prolonged touches; sharing sights, sounds, smells, and opinions; and smiles—one after another, all these give me more joy than ever before. I am starting to understand people stuff more. I get jokes, sarcasm, curiosity, empathy, warmth, and indifference better with each passing day. Obviously, it is difficult for a mermaid to learn how to ride a bike. In the past when I fell off, I did not get back on. Now, I dust myself off and try again. The trusted people helping to hold me up by the bike seat are patient. I hope they are right—"Once you learn how, you never forget."

Practical Implications

1. Homework—SS and I have found it helpful to give each other a topic to mentally consider before our next meeting. This facilitates our conscious and unconscious minds naturally considering the issue while experiencing seemingly unrelated sensations and activities during the time between sessions. We find it

most efficacious to have the topic of focus be as specific as possible. The periodic "aha" moments that result are downright fun and energizing.

2. Downtime—Respect autistic downtime. I assure you there is more going on than meets the walkie-talkie's eye.

3. Try it—Helen Keller claimed she often left her body to experience travel, and no one ran her out town on a rail. Give us the benefit of the doubt. Better yet—lighten up, literally, and try it.

4. Seriousness—Don't take yourself or anyone else too seriously. It seems to chain one up to a stake in a small dirt yard.

5. Best policy—Be honest and don't fret over the consequences of doing so.

6. Hush—Monks are onto something. Silence can open worlds of knowing.

7. Rush less.

8. Learn—Read everything Stephen Hawking writes. He is a smart mute who does not take himself too seriously.

9. By design—remember, being incorporeal is natural and joyous. "As a man is, so he sees." William Blake

10. Consider your favorite color. Children seem to be less detached from their memories of all we are and are capable of enjoying. They have favorite colors for very good reasons.

11. Hypnosis—Lately, SS and I have been starting some sessions with a brief hypnosis exercise in which I relax and disassociate from my physical body and focus my unconscious mind on whatever I choose to work on that day (e.g., body control, vocal control, creativity, humor, recall, clarity, etc.) I thoroughly enjoy it. I find it very relaxing, easy, and effective. Silly SS was surprised at how quickly I could go into trance. Hypnosis is just another hallway which leads to the portal, and I really know my way around there. We found something that I am really good at. Hmmm, it might be a step weirder than belonging to the chess team, and I am fairly sure there are no trophies to be had, but maybe matching T-shirts? A girl can dream.

Smiling Sadist victims: Barb and Ty

Chapter 9

A Girl and Her Horse

Girls—especially young, adolescent ones—have a penchant for making bonds with horses. I am and was no exception. I have been giving this theory a great deal of thought of late, as that is what I do in between battling daily tasks made monumental challenges by my autistic brain's gift of apraxia and ataxia: I sit around and think. Don't get me wrong, I would not trade in my particular hunk of gray matter for any more efficient model. No way. It took me the better part of thirty years to master juggling my ineffable, autistic brain fires. The igniting flares can come from any number of sources. My senses are often so intense and pain soaked you wouldn't believe me even if I described them in the most benign candy-coated way. Or the moment's inferno may have its genesis from a body wired so kooky that it may comply with my request to have a finger push elevator button #2 one day and totally rebel the next, having my limbs shame me with messy incoordination or violent outbursts. Even my speech is controlled by a source outside of my assessable control panel. Countless systems encased in my body operate in open defiance to eons of evolutionary expertise in designing central nervous systems that communicate in tandem. Perpetual, internal contradiction, frustration, and friction tender my indigenous fires.

Autistic fire juggling is not for the faint of heart. My life in the circus as a juggler is difficult, but I am finally getting good at it and I refuse to stop until I hear the crowd cheer in unison. That day may be a long time coming, but I am patient and am now more equipped with tricks of the trade. Gracious and wise horses granted me apprenticeship so that I could practice and learn these secrets.

My theory is that horses are eager teachers of one of the most profound universal truths: peace and happiness are available for the taking, but far too often humans lose sight of where to grab because opaque perspectives camouflage access. I think many girls are exposed to this message on countless saddled backs across the planet. More so than boys, girls make emotionally thick friendships with horses. I can speak only for the estrogen childhood experience today, because I have not done enough male mind squatting to be well versed on the boy's perspective. Who knows what a puppy dog tail component adds to their makeup? But, I assume boys who have the opportunity to ride and commune with horses maintain some emotional distance from the beast due to some testosterone-oiled and evolutionarily sound strength, competition, and dominance posturing. Until I have more firsthand experience in the boy psyche, I will reserve the focus of this discussion to young females.

It is my feeling that little girls in general do not relinquish much brain space to convincing others that they are mighty and right. The wisdom of universal equality reveals that we are all ephemerally frail and at the same time are fueled with immutable power. "Might makes right" posturing fades memory of the truths of universal equality. Therefore, girls often have access to more borderless communication. Also, like me, they listen to everything and discreetly view peripheral happenings and are not credited for doing so by most people.

I intuited early on that horses are beautifully designed for borderless communication. When I was quite young, I thought horses were so large in order to keep all the thoughts, stories, and fears that people like me gave to them. I was no ingrate; I always asked my steed if I could put my current mental waste in that particular horse's receptacle. Never was I denied a sincere request to leave my poison with the munificent beast. Horses are incredibly useful in many ways, but funk disposal is one of their most honed skills. God designed horses with big picture recall that permits equestrian animals to filter and process emotional tar out of separate consciousness. The end product of this waste management is clean, clear energy, which is funneled back into the universal pool.

Recently while atop Zena, one of my favorite horses at Shangri La, I inquired about the process.

The not-so-old mare kept her steady pace and smiled. She voicelessly shared that she had never been asked that or anything else pertaining to her horsy abilities by any of the humans she served. Zena assumed people were all too self-centered to bother thinking about the horse's take on waste management or anything else. She went on to convey that, quite frankly, most humans were not even aware of the recycling they were directly benefiting from. I let her know that I, too, am as self-absorbed as the next *Homo sapien,* but I am aware of the process and curious about all aspects.

This is when it gets interesting, because when I say horses talk to you, they don't really, because the exchange does not involve words. I think this is why I had such relaxing and lovely experiences with horses even before I began to think in words at age nineteen. Zena answered my question this way: she allowed me to dwell in her mind to know firsthand how she conducted her important work. Heretofore, our communication had been one-sided. I donned my fashionable black helmet and boots to protect my delicate humanness, straddled her muscular auburn back, grabbed the reins for show, and sent her my troubles. For the first several years, I sent her—or whatever horse was on duty that day—mental images. Like copying a movie from one DVD to another, I transferred all manner of painful life clips—from countless exclusions; intensely confusing sensory floods; sleepless nights pervaded by self-pity; terrifying daydreams I conjured about losing my parents, making me unfathomably alone; and so much meanness and anger it embarrasses me to recall it. The horse would send nothing back except an intangible receipt, letting me know that my dirty shipment was received. I gave the process no thought, but I do recall being decent enough to thank the beast for a relaxing ride. In my early anxiety-ridden life, moments of peace and release were few and far between. I would be back for more.

These days, I am careful not to become too dependent on my equestrian pals. No need to be like those with disposable incomes who twice weekly trek to the high colonic specialist for cleansing in lieu of eating a few apples and taking a walk. Well, okay, I do enjoy disposable income and trek to the immaculate stables twice a week. But I try daily to incorporate what I learned from Zena. I am getting better at recycling my own funk. I write it down and away. It burdens no landfills, because by the time my editing is done and humor is inserted so the mess will be palatable, the funk has altered states and may now be useful to others toying with self-pity and other ills of perspective. Who knows—maybe someday I can receive loads from other people to help out these gracious, four-legged sanitation workers. For now, I simply clean my own stall. All the world is a circus…and what would a circus be without horses?

Practical Implications

1. See for yourself. Seek a horse-riding experience. I suggest you ride as independently as possible. Other humans chatting at while you are trying to connect with the horse is annoying and counterproductive. The goal

is to not be with other people at this moment but to be…just be…and let the horse be with you. Any exchange of thoughts will happen naturally, as that is the part of *being* that Descartes got right. Remember the old joke? Bartender to Descartes: "Would you like another drink?" Descartes: "I think not"…and then he disappeared.

2. Do not pre-medicate with logic before the experience. You get no prize for figuring the improbability of such a surreal experience. The prize is the surreal experience. Be open to it.

3. Peace and happiness are apples on high branches. Wiggle free from the weighted reins of self-pity and "might makes right." Then balance and quietly reach. Savor the fruit.

A girl and her horse. Life is perspective.
(From top to bottom: Bess, my friend and weekend personal attendant,
and Moon Pie)

Chapter 10

Nothing New Around the Sun

I have a lot on my mind. Turns out I am thirty pounds overweight—again—and my trainer has been talking with me about adjusting my diet and keeping a daily log of my consumption. That is all fine and good, as I enjoy conversing with him. The longer we chat, the less time is allotted for death marches and ab crunches. The problem is, he actually sat down and mapped it all out. He sent me an eleven-page e-mail of calorie—and nutrition-tallied food choices. The plan, which I naively agreed to during one of our procrastination gab sessions, was for me to consume only fourteen hundred calories a day. A fine conversational commitment, but in reality that involves air sandwiches, couscous, enough water to drown coral, and something called *bulgur*. The latter sounds slightly better than it tastes.

Like my fat cells, which keep betraying me by inflating when I indulge myself, my conscience festers up guilt more often than I would like of late. Guilt. Yeah, I think it is guilt. That sneaky character flashes through my life like an unattractive streaker making me look. The peripheral invasion usually occurs just when I am lulling myself with blissfully content experiences like swimming under my thick, soft comforter, enjoying my hunt for evasive cool parts. Yesterday, pesky Guilt sauntered by as I was sitting in a hot tub considering yet another trip to the Olive Garden. I was mentally replaying the crunchy, fresh, tangy, buttery, yeasty satisfactions so dependable in the endless bread sticks and salad, when Guilt changed the rules. He stopped. He stared. "What?" I sassed, perturbed at the blatant interruption. "I see you. Move along." Nothing. He just kept looking at me with patience and superiority. Ewe, I hate that! I fear that this standoff may end in me having to take action, and I have grown so accustomed to saving my action energy for hedonism. The weight—pow, he put it on me. Now I have to do something. Apparently, I am convicted of underachieving. My sentence is to be revealed to me daily. I can choose to be on the lamb, but know the law will always catch up to me.

Guilt tells me I must start thinking on things not just for my own pleasure and curiosity, but in order to help others.

Why not start big? I began to give it the old college try and attempted to find truths concerning the meaning of life, the existence of God and/or the flavor of God, and even the possibility of the framework of a heaven or afterlife just for good measure.

It should be noted that I was raised Catholic, so I recognized Guilt right away. I fared rather well in that religion as a mute autistic presumed to be profoundly retarded until age nineteen. The lamb's share of the Catholic experience—which lays the good citizen foundation of charity, atonement, sacrifice, invaluable guilt, and a ready-made paradigm to answer all that ails ya concerning the precise order of things and how one should behave, complete with levels of consequences for every conceivable behavior permutation—is set by the early teens. My profoundly retarded status made the indoctrination process easy. I was not required to practice my religion or else pay eternal consequences, because, word is, Jesus gives a pass to perpetual intellectual toddlers. It seems the mentally challenged are grandfathered into heaven and need not bother with purgatory middle management and the like.

For me, Church was a delight. Structure and predictability give me comfort. Stained glass makes the morning sun just plain exciting. Rhythmic chants fit in nicely with my mental décor and complement my perpetual rocking. I often blissfully lose myself in the hypnotic dance of candle flames. I have always been fascinated by history and get absorbed in stories of the past. Red wine and bread remain my favorite snacks of all time. And the music? Well, let's just say it moves me deeply in many colors and dimensions. I felt warm, safe, and entertained in church. While neurotypical beings surrounding my homey pew perch dwelled on whether a nap would be possible in the afternoon, what the wait would be at Applebee's if they did not dawdle after mass and avoided asking Mrs. Grainger how she was doing, and intermittent spiritual thoughts, I was left undisturbed to experience and interact with the tame environment. I sniffed hair spray, smoke residue, body odor, gasoline, oily wood; felt the air injecting from a local vent; received the heat from close bodies; and eagerly anticipated the passing of the plate—when I could hold, if only for a moment, the chilly stainless steel while I caressed the regions of warmth dissipating from the last person's touch. I love people-watching, too. So, church was the best show in town—all the stimulation and none of the guilt or responsibility.

Plus, Dad, my favorite person on the planet, took me. In those days, I perceived Mom to be more an extension of my enigmatic self rather than a separate entity. Dad was not ashamed of me, either. I got a divine pass of acceptance with my earthly father, too. His umbrella of confidence and means kept me safe, dry, and well treated. It still does. The Jesus umbrella designed to levitate me and other slightly damaged hangers-on to heaven in Mary Poppins-like fashion is something I wonder about these days. Do I still have a ticket to ride?

I realize that it is unusual for a thirty-six-year-old to be furiously pondering—like it was a contest—the meaning of life, the existence of and flavor of God, and the possibility of a framework for a heaven or afterlife. At this point, folks have usually decided what they believe and are waking up early at least once a week to make sure their little ones buy in to it, too. But I had a rather lengthy moratorium on personal responsibility. The problem is my parents, friends, and especially my psychologist think I am capable of more...much more. If God feels the same way, I have some explaining to do.

I have been working on these conundrums for months, and I can't say that I have made much progress. Of course, it took me years to discern my personhood, too. Autism can put some real roadblocks in processing efficiency. Sometimes, humans are so small. We live life barely knowing anything. I get tired of being so small. The tragedy—or perhaps the greatest blessing (my verdict is still out on that too)—is that the greatest minds have not fared much better. I read Christian, Hindu, Buddhist, and Muslim theologies and studied Plato, Pythagoras, Augustine, Descartes, Spinoza, Einstein, and Hawking. Prominent leaders and followers of the aforementioned theologies, as well as these deep-thinking, extraordinarily intelligent, and driven individuals, have written persuasively on the topics.

In Holton's (2002) article in *Daedalus,* he recounts Einstein's 1929 telegraphed response to Rabbi Herbert S. Goldstein, who asked if he believed in God. "I believe in Spinoza's God, who reveals himself in the lawful harmony of the world, not in the God who concerns Himself with the fate and the doings of mankind." All right, Einstein, we are all human and are drawn to speak the language of our time, but no way can I accept that God is a man (i.e., "Himself"). I figure no way is God a he or a she. God is God. At the very least, God is both—all permutations of sex and gender. Plus, originally, I was not thrilled with not having a personal God who cares about me. So I got to thinking and considering how easy a more comforting philosophy would be to rationalize and own.

Personally, I seem to remember, or at least feel instinctively comfortable with, my belief that we are all flecks of God. This is backed by Spinoza's proof structure in *Ethics,* which states, "No substance can be produced or created by anything other than itself." Is that enough to call it a day, pursue my life purpose (which I may have made up my own self), and sleep well at night? Perhaps. If I am secure with the God belief, and I am, the real challenge remaining is: "So now what?" Does that mean each creature has a purpose, and does God care about "the fate and doings of mankind"?

Consider a spring Saturday filled with sunshine and children playing in the yard with a nebulous understanding that they came from their parents, and while the folks set up some rules, they are pretty much on their own devices until the supper bell rings. Is that what we are dealing with here? Maybe.

I'll borrow a couple of lines from Samuel Beckett's play, *Waiting for Godot;*

Estragon: "I can't go on like this."

Vladimir: "That's what you think."

God cares about us all through us all. This thought occurred to me while I was in a bar and grill and as all the televisions showed sports: sports highlights, sport talk shows, sporty commercials, and every kind of game or contest imaginable. I took a good look at bull riding. Ouch. It never seems to work out well. It occurred to me that I do not have the slightest interest in bull riding, while it is obviously a passion for many. I was, however, riveted to a brief segment the on-demand cable preview box almost accidentally showed a clip of Alice Walker discussing how she developed her extraordinary novel *The Color Purple.* SS refers to this phenomenon of different strokes for different folks as "hot rods and gazebos." She can't wrap her mind around why anyone would spend time and money adding flashy paint and gadgets to an old car, only to make it gaudy and still not as efficient or fast as new cars. It's the same with gazebos—what is the point of having a covered deck in the middle of the yard?

My point is everybody cares about something or someone. I think God does, too. By design, God's ingenious plan of heredity makes permutations constant with every generation, which leads to evolution and bull riders, gazebo owners, a puppy licking the wounds of its slightly damaged sibling, and other such pockets of direct care and interest.

What if the way God cares for all the needs of all creatures across all time is by the system itself, not periodic deistic interventions initiated by a prayer request or sacrifice? The system is designed in such a way that all life forms are invested and thus care about life—another life or their own. The former covers sharks, as I was hard pressed to surmise any empathetic tendency. Then it occurred to me that they, at the very least, must care for their own survival. There—see, someone cares even if it is you caring for just your own shark self. So, is God concerned, as Einstein put it, "with the fate and doings of mankind"? Yes. If God created the universe and all that is in it, and as Spinoza points out in *Ethics,* "No substance can be produced or created by anything other than itself," then we are all God, or at lest part of God.

So, does praying help? I will get back to that.

You see, the meaning of life and whether or not God is concerned with the affairs of the created must be linked to the workings of the mind from which the universe sprang. What does that mind want? Sports, comedy, love, good books, a warm hut, religious freedom, health, food, worship, obedience—what?

My parents and I all have quite different perceptions of church. We all had considerably different formative life experiences. Dad was in the military, Mom was a military brat, and I was just a brat.

Dad holds a deep sense of community and worries about the future. Mom is fiercely independent, compartmentalized, and practical. She is not godless, but rather action oriented and efficient. Actually, I am not certain it is possible to be "godless." Can any fleck of God be without its primary component? I think not. Anyway, for Mom, putting on uncomfortable clothes and sitting still in a pew an hour each week listening to a poor, caste man explain how everything is…is not Mom's idea of a good use of time. Mom lives in the here and now—beautifully guilt free. I am sure she will fare just as well in the hereafter. Mom might be surprised to acknowledge just how many times she does invoke God. True, it is often on the eighteenth hole. But she is fully aware and appreciative many moments of many days. Mom allows herself to be awestruck with nature and human achievement, also often on the eighteenth hole. At any rate, she feels, loves, and emanates God. Church was just a little too contrived and team oriented for Mom. Plus, growing up, Dad could be counted on to take me to church. Mom stayed home. For a woman who donned me as her Tasmanian devil sidekick 24/7 for years on end, mass probably meant a spiritual blessing of a little peace and cherished alone time.

Dad's church experience was much more provincial. I fear he may consider me an infidel—or an iconoclast at the very least—after reading this piece. I hope not. I seek not to obviate anyone's working beliefs or proselytize to my austere stew of proposed axioms. I am just writing out loud, as it helps me to understand what is known and what is not.

It is my prayer that we each listen to and observe the God in us and others. When we study such God particles, we are better able to understand the God gestalt. That understanding leads to generosity of spirit. Generosity of spirit is prayer. Prayer is focusing appreciation and reverence and positively requesting from all that is God, blessings for self and others. Does such prayer work? I think so. I believe so. And I am not alone in those thoughts and beliefs. That's what makes it work. It feels natural, if not innate.

Like all else, prayer is a gift of the system. God cannot be separated from the system.

Thus, the purpose of life is to experience God and all that God entails.

Practical Implications

1. Look for God. Listen for God. Be a God detector. Smile and give warm thanks when you sense God. Soon, you will be blanketed in God. Loneliness becomes a silly toy marketed to distracted souls.

   The mind, the Buddha, living creatures—these are not three different things.

   Avatamasaka Sutra

2. Avoid hubris. It is the human trap. Enjoy the God wrap but know that you are an energy blip of the infinite natural power of all that is, was, and ever will be.

   Roses under my window make no reference to former roses or to better ones; they are for what they are; they exist with God today. There is no time to them. There is simply the rose; it is perfect in every moment of existence

   Ralph Waldo Emerson

97

3. Be generous in spirit because that is who you are. It is who we all are if we just recall.

4. Guilt is illumination. Guilt serves to highlight what is not part of our generous-in-spirit selves.

5. Prayer is generosity of spirit and may manifest in internal and external action. Prayer is designed to lead to peace and justice.

6. A few words on justice: Justice almost always takes considerable gestation and pain to birth. Let's continue to midwife each other on our various labors. Our lives may be blessed with bouncing justice born quick, but we must continue to push.

In this moment, I am enjoying a tour of the rain forests in Costa Rica. In this moment, a family goes to sleep with the sorrow of their young children finding their old yellow lab died that evening only to awake to the truth that their beloved 17 year old daughter lost her battle with cancer before dawn. In this moment, an 8 year-old text messages his Granny that he loves her and if he had one wish it would be that she was "immortal". In this moment, a Palestinian laborer blinded by a grenade meant for others gropes dirty walls to find a passage leading to the rumored line for United Nations powdered milk for his fading babies. In this moment, a frail human understands the peace that comes from impermanence and commits to lifting others and self now and forever.

Barb's Introduction

Presenting introductions in the middle of the book makes perfect sense to late bloomers and unconventional thinkers.

I am thirty-nine years old and I can't speak, but plenty of strange sounds and bizarre Touretts-like phrases come out of my busy mouth. I have significant trouble controlling my body. I appear incompetent to stand trial. Luckily, I am charged only with Autism at this time...and I have a doctor's note for that. I can type unassisted these days but it is very slow, perhaps one word per thirty seconds. But I practice daily to improve that. My main method of typing is with warm human support to stabilize my hand or wrist to help me initiate striking letter by letter on an oversized keyboard. This process is called Facilitated Communication (FC) or Supported Typing (ST) or perhaps Bull Shit (BS) if you hail from the camp of skeptics who don't think I am in here. I am not here to convince you that I am here. I am here that you may hear, "I Might Be You."

My boorish movements and incessant ungovernable speaking of nonsensical phrases make me appear to be someone you don't want to know because it would be way too much trouble. To the untrained eye and often, especially to the trained eye, my presentation confirms "Whoa, a majorly disabled creature here with surly precious little intellect!" My company causes curiosity and suspicion, but rarely attraction and never respect. Hmmm, attraction and respect are perhaps what I desire most. Let's explore this ironic phenomenon.

I don't know that devastation hit me; it simply became me at about two-and-a-half years old. I have Autism. Autism has me. A permanent coven. Prior to that, I was precocious and very attractive, the apple of my family's eye. Then, POW! All Rentenbach eyes were blackened.

Autism is the gift that keeps on giving—24/7. Gifts like these are why the Better Business Bureau was created. It is not what you ordered. Everybody wants to take it back; most want to sue. But the company is long gone. You're stuck with it.

My stoic Mom tried to make the best of it—of me. She did not dwell long on who sent this putrid gift or why. No use shooting the messenger either. Note to Mom from the Stork: "Here is your third child—the beautiful, healthy girl you always wanted. Well, not exactly...horseshoes and hand grenades... Gotta fly, S."

Mom is a resilient military brat who always lands on her feet and is not one to look back or ruminate. She finds doing so simply pushes the pause button on the life she is trying to live. Mom understands impermanence not in the same way Dad does with his engineering mind and faith-filled heart. Mom gets it by enjoying the now. Her bouncing baby Tasmanian daughter made enjoying the now extraordinarily difficult for a good quarter of a century.

I describe in *Synergy*, the raw emotions of living with autism and being unable to communicate or deal with the sensory bombardments that electrocute every few minutes. Like a death row inmate already in the chair who gets jolted to find it was only a dream, but to his horror—one that never ends.

None of it made since. I clearly remember being fat, sassy, and carefree. Okay, in reality I am fat now, but was not then, making this all even more upsetting.

Before the autism revolution, I had words, slept well, and was able to make my body play fair. I smiled often. That would be taken, too, just for good measure. I enjoyed lots of welcome hugs—the kind where grinning grown folk effortlessly scooped me up and squeezed me securely, often with a lively spin and a gourmet sniff of my warm sugar cookie toddler essence. The joy of hugging was one of the first things to go.

My tree was pruned quickly but a branch at time.

I was just getting started and loving life, then one day an explosion knocked me off my tiny feet. Knowing nothing of electrical storms and roadside bombs, I simply got shell-shocked and started freaking out, expecting another peripheral explosion.

The detonations began getting more frequent, fierce, and closer. War closed in. Like any child would, I shut up, hid, and rocked in terror.

Soon, the electrical blasts were not flanking me…they were in me. What was me and what was autism? Enemy take over? Enemy is me? I lost language. How did that happen?

My beautiful spring bounty of word tulips froze. Each succumbed to the bizarre frost—and shattered. Only gloriously colored word remnants remained scattered with cruel abandon on the hard earth. Pronouns were the first to die. They had no meaning. Pronoun death brought a drought of associations. From there, thinking ceased to build upon itself. Nothing came easy but chaos, confusion, and fear.

When I lost language, everything changed. A cold, electrically charged mist shrouded my personhood. I lost me. It would be almost two decades before I caught another good glimpse of myself in the fog, but the adorable child was gone.

At age two and one half, frigid Autism and I became one country.

Autism is a cold communist state. I sensed a faceless, aloof dictator but no God. Prayers could not penetrate the iron curtain. Communications were severed. Travel was forbidden. I was alone. I was scared. Nothing worked well. My own senses and body betrayed me. I was stuck. Hope for a better life faded.

My anger and resentment to God was the only thing that grew in this gray land.

When I had the energy, I blindly attacked everything and everybody. When I tired, I tried to close my twitching posttraumatic stress disorder eyes and float away. Such brief ethereal escapes were always soured by opening my eyes to the confines of Autism again.

Dual citizenship was not easy to negotiate, but I persevered. Learning the language of both countries was my start. This cold block alliance lasted until I was nineteen years old and was freed by facilitated communication. While I was a minor, Autism ruled the land. But at nineteen, I recovered words and my Cold War was over. I began typing. I regained personhood and worked out a dual citizenship with Autism and myself.

Some changes were immediate...other vestiges from Autism's icy grip still bind me.

In the following chapters, I will do my best to share some of what I learned about how to work out a diplomatic resolution with autism so that others may also find freedom and warmth. I will speak of SS, which stands for "smiling shrink," my nickname for educational psychologist Dr. Lois Prislovsky, who, over the past ten years, has helped me negotiate treaties with Autism and everyone else.

Sincerely, Logophile B

At Forty, I am no longer alone and Jerry and I see the mountaintop.

Introduction by Lois

I saw a twenty-three-year-old woman for a hypnosis appointment designed to treat her dermatillomania (compulsive skin picking). The session was successful. She noted on the feedback form: *The most difficult part of this session was—* "telling a stranger personal thoughts and feelings." Traditional psychology is all about describing and analyzing problems and finding causes, so to tailor the hypnosis to her individual needs and maximize connotations, it is necessary to get an understanding of the details and depth of her impulse control problem. Thus, on the first session, I unceremoniously ask very personal questions about relationships, urges, obsessive thoughts, substance use, fears, and anxieties. We practitioners expect our clients to disclose almost automatically and never share our own selves.

My role in this book is different. **This book is about equality and connecting**. Barb and I share private thoughts and feelings in hopes of breaking down barriers to promote collaborative equality with families, practitioners, and individuals with ASD.

How can I ask my clients to be authentic and fight through discrimination to be their highest selves if I am unwilling to?

On that note, I mention our dear son, Elijah (E), now age twelve, whose brain is in that epic stage of effortless learning, which has much to do with plasticity and not drinking beer. He often offers his fresh perspective on my work so it won't come off "all preachy teachy." Some people make the best out of life while others get stuck and never move past the hard parts. This book presents strategies to avoid such muck blocks. Some theories are less worthy of a book than others, but E is always a candid and active coscientist. We often brush our teeth, play

Frisbee, racquet ball, ping-pong, etc., with our left hands so if we ever have a stroke, we are ahead of the game. I also have him pee on the garden (houseplants are spared), which we theorize has little to do with stroke rehabilitation but may be an organic fertilizer. Seems all that creatinine, sodium, potassium, magnesium, calcium, ammonium, phosphates, sulfates, and puppy dog tails supercharge because we had tomato plants the size of our Prius and the peppers kept growing well into December. We wash off the pee.

Children teach much as they live free and strong. **Children are easily themselves and thus are happy and resilient. As we age away from who we were born to be, we sometimes fall into the trap of thinking that the solution to the problem lies outside of ourselves. We hope these writings will jog memories of you and from there you will mindfully connect with others.** Thinking is linking.

Einstein called this kind of thinking "combinatorial play." It is using imagination to mix concepts to create new associations. Some call it "thinking outside the box." Einstein's exact words were, "the search for patterns that yield new meanings." When Elijah was six, on the first day we got to enjoy the pool at our new home, we envisioned combining two of our favorite activities (riding bikes and skate boarding) with his most favorite activity, swimming (I am a big fan of swimming, too, but discovered great sex a few years ago.). Five minutes later, we took turns riding his bike underwater. It really works! So does skateboarding...although it is much slower. I was almost forty years old and it never occurred to me that one could ride a bike in a swimming pool (Oh, unicycles work, too.). Now, we know. **And now, I am smart enough to pay much more attention to individuals with fresh perspectives.**

In fact the title of this book, *I Might Be You* came from such a lad. Fifteen-year-old AB was in session with me and doing a sentence completion self-expression exercise when he filled in the blank with "you" to this stem, "I might be _____." Wow! At the time, AB was mostly non-verbal, very aggressive, and struggled mightily with any type of word generation, but this succinct production spoke volumes about what he wished to communicate.

This book is about being your strongest self by connecting with others, so we may piggyback and gain perspective to see more, know more, do more, be more, and serve more. "If I have seen further than others, it is by standing upon the shoulders of giants." Isaac Newton

Combinatorial players Barb, Mel, Aidan, Elijah, Lois, and Charlie

Chapter 11

Friends: Ticket to Ride

In the first part of this book, I wrote a chapter on friendships with conviction. In this section, I again write on friendships, but this time with different conviction. As Webster shares one then two uses of conviction, "1.) State of mind in which one is free from doubt. And 2.) Idea that is believed to be true or valid without positive knowledge," so do I.

I was free from doubt, now I am free to believe.

I accept the idea that social connection leads to cooperation and makes success practicable.

John Donne wrote, "No man is an island, entire of itself; every man is a piece of the continent, a part of the main; any man's death diminishes me, because I am involved in mankind; And therefore never send to know for whom the bell tolls; It tolls for thee.

As an autistic, I have not always been involved in mankind. Man has not always been kind to me. To be fair, I have not always been the effervescent beauty pageant poster child spending her only wish on world peace. My swimsuit interview would have been damning, as my autistic sash would do little to hide the girth of my anger and thighs.

Before words reinstated my personhood passport in 1992, I was very much an island and wrote of my non-irenic volcanic state in Part one: Synergy.

Martin Nowak and Rodger Highfield in *Supercooperators: Altruism, Evolution, and Why We Need Each Other to Succeed* describe how actively pursuing the "snuggle for existence" is the key to survival as a species. Now they tell me.

Do you know what life is without friends? Not much, I tell you.

Humans are a companionable species and need friends. People with autism are human and thus need friends. Help! But we auts must first ready ourselves. Like the old joke of a guy praying with vigor everyday at the altar for years on end that God would let him win the lottery. Finally, beleaguered Jesus shook free from his crucifixion statue and exclaimed, "Okay, okay, but buddy, please buy a ticket!"

Words are the ticket.

A couple of years ago, a friend, my first totally "nonpaid," threw me the lifeline because I had the ticket to ride. I instinctively grabbed and hung on for my not so dear life. I was thirty-six and I did not possess a noetic understanding of friendship; only the word was familiar to me.

Shakespeare's Tragic Juliet teaches us over 400 years ago that it is dangerous to play possum…and what matters is what something is, not what it is called.

JULIET: 'Tis but thy name that is my enemy;
Thou art thyself, though not a Montague.
What's Montague? It is not hand, nor foot,
Nor arm, nor face, nor any other part
Belonging to a man. O, be some other name!
What's in a name? That which we call a rose
By any other name would smell as sweet;
So Romeo would, were he not Romeo call'd,
Retain that dear perfection which he owes
Without that title. Romeo, doff thy name,
And for that name which is no part of thee
Take all myself.

For many of us Autistics, society has thrown around the word "friend" to refer to other kids in our special (the kind of special that no one wants to be) classes, preferred caregivers, fellow sun baked auts at well-meaning summer camps, guilt free peer mentors, and even our teachers and principals. Remember the cutsie lil spelling tip our instructors bounced about how to differentiate the homophones: principle and principal with the latter being our pal? Bullshit.

My new conviction is that "friendly" is quite distinct from "friend." People may or may not have been friendly to me; the latter often depended upon who was around to see (a nonmute "who" witness of course). Now, I feel what a friend is. "Friendly" is not it. In his book, *To Know as We Are Known*, Parker describes this revelation as a natural manifestation of the interaction between the knowers and the known: "We now see that to know something is to have a living relationship with it—influencing and being influenced by the object known." I should note a fun mystical connection here—Parker's exceptional book just plopped on my ample lap today as I was making the finishing touches on this chapter. It was a gift from my second totally nonpaid friend, Elizabeth. Boo!

Romeo does retain that dear perfection. Allow me to describe genuine souls who seek out and enjoy my company, whose love and connection perfection I feel rather than simply label them with the weakened term, "friend."

You see, over the last two years, I gained true acceptance from not one, but two neurotypical cohorts. They are not damaged goods, either. Each, about my age, is physically attractive, very educated, and delightful. The purity is that these two buddies connect with me under our own steam. **Obligation fuels no part of our bond**. They are not paid or service providers for me in any way or tied to my family. Our only roles are to enjoy each other and have each other's back (Evolutionarily most beneficial.).

How did this happen? Here is my best guess.

They read my work.

I wrote, "Evolution has not wired all of us to attain such relationships easily. Some humans do not give having friends much thought—it just happens naturally. One top-heavy toddler hugs the tiny neck of another. From there, they battle with sharing and acquire language and exchange it as a limitless commodity."

Like cheap oil in Dubai, words fuel friendships and that vital product is taken for granted by the indigenous. Not being from the land of cheap words, Autistics have a very hard time making nonpaid friends. But I finally did it at age thirty-six by getting words (and lots of them) out there. Then two beings were able to relate to me in a new way.

My slick words were expensive and time consuming to excavate. It is hard to find good help in dystopia, but I did. SS helped me drill down and find my crude words. The refinement process took years.

Eventually, my product was ready for market. In *Synergy* and other publications, I shared my past, humor, dreams, flaws, and interests. The same stuff you normals do on your first friend date. Jessica liked what she read and contacted me for a chat. After a few e-mail correspondences, I was able to establish my footing. I began to understand that she was not seeking something from me —but seeking me. It took time to acclimate. I was incredulous at first. Jessica was a Ph.D. student in educational psychology—same field as SS. I fished, but reeled in no evidence that she wanted to study or treat me. Curious. Surely this gal had many good friends. And Jessica is simply not the gold digger type. I can divine that vein a mile away. What did she want? Should I open the door? After eliminating a series of possible motives, I calculated the worse case scenario was she is another cloyingly pious God Squad activist who believes Hell does not discriminate against mute autistics and is making sure no salvation rock has been left unturned. I did not allow myself to entertain a best-case scenario. So, fortified with my most powerful religious arguments, I met Jessica at SS'ss office for a face-to-face so I could communicate with FC.

We had a riveting conversation. Turns out religion was a topic, but that may be more my doing since I was prepared to spar. We met like this a couple of times. Jessica never did give me a *Watchtower* pamphlet, instruct me on how to accept Jesus in my heart, or ask for a donation. We simply began to share aspects of our lives, along with plenty of good food, wine, and music. "Simply," is an interesting word choice for something that took thirty-six years to happen.

After I answered the door for Jessica, Elizabeth came a knocking. She also visits with no agenda other than mutual interests, affinity, and dare I say it, ...friendship. A girl could get used to this and I have. Another friendship followed this one and I see no end in sight as my welcome mat is out. Words don't fail me now. The rose smells as sweet.

Before Jessica and Elizabeth, I suspect my most practical knowledge of what friendship is was by knowing what it is not. I picked up this approach from negative theology, which is an attempt to achieve unity with the Divine Good through discernment, gaining knowledge of what God is *not*, rather than by describing what God *is*.

The gist of negative theology or apophasis is that God is so far beyond human understanding and experience that the only hope we have of getting close to the nature of God is to list what God definitely is not.

I did this with Jessica before we met. After each e-mail exchange, I mentally tallied what she might bring and what I would turn away as not friend.

In his "About.com Guide" article, Austin Cline traces this negative theology to Christianity in the late fifth century by an anonymous author. Even earlier, Cappadocian Fathers of the fourth century deduced that while they believed in God, they did not believe that God exists. This was because the very concept of "existence" inappropriately applied positive attributes to God.

The premise of negative theology is that nothing positive and definite can be said about the nature of reality because it is beyond knowing. That is where I was before Jessica and Elizabeth. **The good news is like God, friendship may be beyond knowing, but it is not beyond feeling.**

I feel God.

I feel Friendship.

Now, to figure out what is God and what is Friend.

Practical Implications:

1. Share books, articles, poems, and videos with friends. Learning the same stuff weaves a stronger connection.

2. If you don't wish to write a book, consider blogging or keeping a journal of your perspectives. The process of thinking through it to yourself will help you communicate your perspectives to others when the time is right.

Non-paid friends: Barb, Jessica, and Elizabeth

Chapter 12

Connection—That's the Ticket

Barb and I have worked together for over ten years. Her consistent strides toward balance, maturity, and independence have been bolstered by prolific introspective writings, which should assist those who seek a nice perch on her curved shoulders.

A few months ago, Barb was asked by a parent of a teenager with "severe autism" how she began seeing challenges differently. Barb typed, "Like the good people in the seventeenth and eighteenth century enlightenment, I began to 'dare to know.'"

Barb went on to explain that she found freedom via "natural reasoning," which, Descartes assures, can prove theology and is universal. Like John Locke and Emmanuel Kant, Descartes also defends religion by reason (Barb has a passion for history and philosophy and enjoys weaving that knowledge into her daily communications. Thinking is linking.) Barb amended, "Actually, natural reasoning was step two for my path to freedom. Step one was connecting with another. **Once I was not alone, I became bolder.**"

As Barb experienced and subsequently understood pure ("nonpaid") friendships, she shared, "St. Thomas Aquinas, patron of Catholic Education, heralds that God does not step back and watch us but is sustaining the world at all times. Always constantly creating. I believe God is in us all. So we all create, albeit some more mindfully than others. **Each day I create my life a choice at a time**. No longer do I await my fate and have anger as my only reaction. I take action."

By linking her thinking, Barb made real friends.

How can we help those with ASD to become less alone so they, too, may take initiative and design their own lives?

To hear those who do not speak, one must really listen well.

Let them teach us how they know—the what-they-know comes later.

In his book, *To Know as We are Known*, Parker J. Palmer says, "In this kind of education, the relationship between the teacher, the student, and the subject is one of obedience. The word 'obedience' does not mean slavish, uncritical adherence; it comes from the Latin root *audire,* which means 'to listen'. Obedience requires a discerning ear, the ear that listens for the reality of the situation, a listening that allows the hearer to respond to that reality, whatever it may be." Later, Palmer extends this truth seeking from those who are silent: "It allows them to speak their truth to knowers who want to listen obediently, knowers whose aim is not manipulation and mastery but membership in the community of truth."

To date, education is the primary treatment for Autism. There is capacious room for improvement. **The way we teach and treat depends on the way we think clients know.** Effective practitioners are more attentive to what others are trying to communicate with regard to understanding not just what they know, but how they know. **When we connect mindfully with others, we facilitate linking thinking. From there, actions are purposeful and learning is not a one-way street.**

It is okay to be open to changing our empirically sound approaches. Education and psychology are flimsy if static. It does not weaken our "expertise" to make conscious efforts to learn from those we serve. I had a challenging dynamic assessment with a non-verbal fourteen-year-old male (CD) with pronounced autistic symptomology. Quite simply, he refused to participate. At one point, CD put his head down on the table and began to cry with conviction. He increased his self-injurious behaviors (hand and wrist biting—hard), then jammed his index finger in to the bottom of his ear. He bawled and grimaced. I was concerned. I went into the lobby to explain to his father that I thought his son was in genuine pain. His father, one of the most steadfast parents I have ever known, has restructured his life in order to spend the maximum amount of time with CD. He clearly has CD's best interests at heart. His father said, "Oh, this is an avoidance technique." He then proceeded to tell the six-foot, 185-pound child, "I really want to hear that scream. It needs to be louder. And you can bite harder that that. Bite it really hard!" As a more novice practitioner, I may not have been open to such an "unsophisticated" approach as "reverse psychology." But it worked (This was good for myriad reasons—not the least of which is that this took place on a weekday afternoon when our offices were fully booked. Unless one is selling Jack Daniels at a street fight, grown men screaming is rarely good for business.).

Pity is not empowering. I should not have given it. The error was mine. What we know from those we know is—**pity serves no one. Let it go.**

Barb let us know early on that eavesdropping was a significant pathway to her learning. Thus, when one of us is studying with her, it is accepted that as we read aloud, Barb may choose to sit across the room seemingly "in her own world." She may even choose to cover her head with a pillow or jacket. As memory competitors may wear the best noise reduction headphones available and close their eyes while trying to visualize mnemonics to recall the precise order of playing cards or Pi out to 1000 digits, so, too, Barb channels her mental focus by reducing input to her other senses. Then she is able to commandeer more brain real estate than just the temporal lobe to help her process the information fully.

Another client, EF, shows us through his preferred activities that computer navigation is a huge source of knowing for him. Therefore, we create social skills, academic development, and expressive language practices to be woven through his preferred medium via e-mails, Skype, videos, educational gaming, etc. Furthermore, EF enjoys movies and musicals. He recites entire scripts and songs from memory, but struggles to generate novel expressive language. We discovered having EF read the lyrics and sing along with male musical solos (that are new to EF) improves his language production in natural settings.

The front door is not the only way to enter. These people are home.

GH teaches us he learns best through yet another entrance. He codifies what is abstract, associating back to his corporeal realities. With math, for example, we encourage his mastery with use of manipulatives like the abacus, symbolic tokens, giant number lines, and other hands-on calculations to help him conceptualize multiplication, division, square roots, work problems, and algebra. GH then links his thinking, and those neuronal pathways become well traveled and efficient. Abstract mathematics becomes concrete, and as a result, doable.

In hypnosis, I often ask clients during the acclimation visit where they feel most comfortable in their own skin; safe, strong, and whole. Typical answers are "lying on the beach" or "walking through woods." Clients with autism may choose places that teach us much about their vestibular preferences. Swinging, being in their own bed under the covers, swimming, car rides, and horseback riding are common. We find hypnosis to be very effective with our clients with autism, which is not surprising since they are often masters of their interior lives.

Michael Gelb writes in *Discover Your Genius* that a landmark survey of the working methods of great scientists and mathematicians found their thinking processes were not characterized by language or mathematical symbols, but rather by visual imagery. Such was clearly the case with Einstein, who participated in the survey: "The words of language, as they are written or spoken, do not seem to play any role in my mechanisms of thought." Einstein added that his own processes instead "rely, more or less, on clear images of a visual and some of a muscular type."

I believe this is one of the reasons hypnosis exercises with visual and other sensory-guided imagery often works so well with our ASD clients. We use such techniques for anger management, tics, and language production. For example, with the latter, we may help the client remember the experience of speaking when it came easier for them. They may vividly relive the sights, sounds, feelings, environment, what they looked like, and what it felt like to speak. Then, they practice this mentally. Norman Doidge's book, *The Brain that Changes Itself*, accounts research indicating that mental practice can be as effective as physical practice in strengthening neurological pathways. Doidge also notes the role of hemispheric asymmetry, which shows us that most language is in the left hemisphere. Likewise, visualization is most often found in the right hemisphere, but that can change as we can train the brain to lateralize. To maximize neuroplasticity, it may therefore be prudent to encourage clients with autism to cross the hemisphere with exercises that take language from the left side to the right side and vice versa.

Finding out where individuals with autism feel most competent and at ease provides good footing for connection.

Renowned neuroscientist and prolific brain research expert, Michael Merzenich, teaches us that the best way to improve thinking is not by asking people to do what they can't. **Rather, building on abilities is the best path to strengthen weaknesses.**

A few weeks ago, I spent the first fifteen minutes of a session in silence tearing recycled paper into narrow strips. Shredder on the fritz? Nope. I was trying to meet a man by sharing his favorite pastime. IJ is fifteen years old and prior assessments labeled him "profoundly retarded" (one of Barb's diagnoses). He is mostly nonverbal and often exhibits disturbing behaviors at home and school, such as self-injurious behaviors (SIDS), yelling, public masturbation, nose picking (and eating), and a variety of rhythmic gestures to regulate a seemingly overloaded sensory system. **His education to date consisted mainly of ways to keep himself and others safe.** And attempts to teach IJ letters, numbers, colors, etc. had intermittent success. At this time, he was refusing any such remedial work at school or in therapy. His parents have tried "everything" at considerable expense, but nothing has brought relief or progress. When IJ first came to our group, Dr. Jessica Lester and I each worked with IJ once a week. No significant breakthroughs were made...except that Dr. Lester and I concurred that IJ's intellectual capabilities are much higher than assessments reveal. His receptive language is just too refined and his fine and gross motor skills are strong. The dilemma is how to connect with IJ to understand how he learns and hopefully help motivate him to make the consistent effort it takes to find purpose and productivity. We are wise to draw from Nelson Mandela's famous advice on the art of persuasion: "Don't address their brains. Address their hearts," or as Barb astutely noted, **"Many times, autistics revert to isolation by default rather than preference. It is infinitely easier to back**

away and not try to be included, instead of oafishly stepping in and attempting to convey your intent to be a part. *Loneliness is the most predominant side effect of our unique design.*"

My paper tearing was clearly of interest to IJ, but he was slow to join in at first, observing only with his peripheral vision and uncharacteristic quiet. With understated gestures, I offered him some of the paper. IJ finally took me up on shredding. His face softened with smiles and he began to inaudibly whisper happy phrases as we voicelessly shared an activity on equal footing. Not so equal actually, as IJ was noticeably more talented at getting the strips linear. Mine were jagged and lopsided as torn by an armless crocodile. From there, we enjoyed the calmest productive session to date. I respected his time and interest.

He knew I was trying to be with him—not fix him. **That day, we focused on treating isolation, not autism**.

In the weeks that followed, we moved on from paper tearing to other more constructive cooperative play like building molecular models. Eventually, we tapped into his true passion—cooking. So then, I saw IJ in his home where we worked the first half of the session on academic and speech production tasks that he never used to tolerate. The second half of the session, he cooked. IJ beamed as he prepared detailed recipes that he gets to eat. His kitchen, communication, and self-control skills strengthened each week. IJ began taking increased ownership of the sessions and initiated language and physical tenderness. IJ clearly desires to be given the benefit of the doubt about his intelligence. He teaches us this by responding with mature control when treated this way and with disruptive, puerile behaviors when patronized. He now transitions easily from one task to the next and is able to maintain focus for the entire session—unprecedented in his education. He can let yelling, SIDS, banging, inappropriate behaviors, and pacing go as he listens to what is of interest. One could do worse than gain an education through cooking but, that was just the beginning. IJ now works without the cooking carrot and gives his full attention to speech production/regulation and academics for the duration of the session as he sits comfortably at his kitchen table or in my office. As his connections and knowledge grow along side his ability to sustain attention and control his body, a natural hunger for more should ensue.

Barb conveys that a sense of purpose gave her the reason to live. Her writings also let others know who she is, which is difficult for those with Autism to communicate. We "neurotypical walkie talkies" take presenting our persona for granted. Once people outside of her immediate board of trustees discovered her personhood, two genuine "nonpaid friends," Jessica and Elizabeth, appeared.

Perhaps, like a sister more than a psychologist, I began wanting "it" (love and intimate connection with peers) intensely for Barb. I worked with Jessica and Elizabeth and encouraged them to read Barb's stuff. As Barb accounts, that was all it took. After Jessica and Elizabeth read her work, each individually started an e-mail correspondence with Barb. To date, e-mail is Barb's favorite form of communication as it puts her on an even playing field. From there, they began to share social outings and confidences. Those true friendships begot others and Barb now enjoys a full social life, complete with an emerging romantic relationship.

I always speak enthusiastically about Barb and share that she is both a personal friend and a client. It should be noted we professionals are trained this is not best practice, but like a divorce that worked out really well—I would do it again. Barb is perhaps the most interesting person I have ever known. She is complicated, sincere, patient, and talented, with layers of perceptions that unfold like a 4H prize-winning onion. We truly enjoy each other's company. We manage our dual roles simply and honestly by setting clear lines between "sessions" and "friend time." Sessions are scheduled, recorded, and billed. During those times (as with any other client), I am polite, professional, and give Barb my undivided attention to best council and assist in her personal development. Friend time with Barb or any of my other pals is not so structured or refined. Our inner circle is a lively, non-PC crowd and jesting is the sport of choice.

The first "friend" trip we took together was to Costa Rica in 2005. I had just begun a long-term relationship break up and was "graduate-student" poor again. Lucky for me, my prolonged-gratification career choice prepared me well for this reversal of fortune. Basement apartment, two jobs, Ramen noodles, cheap beer, second-hand clothes, no cable...check. My new love, by no coincidence, was also going through the same kind of transition and profound financial regression. Near possession free, emotionally raw but with a clear vision of brighter days, my partner Ty and I came into some unexpected money—aka TAX Refunds (Tax refunds are jubilant lottery wins for the poor.)! By pooling our money, as the poor are happy to do, we had just enough to buy a couple's package to a weeklong surf camp in Costa Rica. It was a dream of mine to learn to surf before I turned forty. Check.

Now, Barb and I had traveled on trips before, but always with a paid component, as I would go to assist her. Well, that is not entirely true as I took Barb as a guest on a UTK Football trip (job perk in my previous position) a few months prior to Costa Rica. But the Cotton Bowl does not count as that was during the peak of the screaming part of my break up and the company of a friendly mute was preferred.

Costa Rica was different. It was a well-needed vacation and we asked Barb if she wanted to go. Now, Barb is no surfer, as her aversion to the granulation of beach sand (it is a texture thing) prevents her from even getting close. But she loves a tropical destination and all that goes with it. Barb is all about fetching cabana boys courting her with complimentary drinks, smiles, and well wishes for Bingo swag. "It would be my pleasure, Ma'am" is one of her favorite phrases—right behind, "More bread sticks?"

One night at a modest dinner out, I was served a fish complete with head and eyeballs. I spooned out one hard orb and told Barb about the fictitious, regional delicacy. She took the spoon, as I knew she would, and proceeded to smell and taste it as she does with everything that is a manageable size. It was so small she inadvertently sucked it in and swallowed the eye without the slightest pause or crunch. Ty was in a separate conversation, but peripherally saw my lying "tell" (apparently, my chin trembles when I am trying to get away with something). Ty lunged across the table in a heroic taking-the-bullet-for-another slow motion save yelling, "Nooooo!" Too late. Barb ate it. Seeing the commotion, the waiter scurried over to explain in broken English, "Eye eating is no good." Barb typed with vigor, "You are dead to me." When my laughing subsided, the rest of the table insisted I eat the other eye. Fortunately, after years of finding bedbugs, quarters, and other valuables behind Elijah's ears and in his armpits—I am rather skilled at slight of hand.

Barb told me later, "That's when I knew I was in." She explained, "One would have to be a real asshole to prank those you pity." Barb began to wield her own brand of pranks and our friendship deepened.

It took months before I realized Barb stole a magazine from the lobby at our offices every time she exited. She is a master at jokes requiring gestation. Barb almost always lowers the windows of my car just a crack as I am turning off the engine. If I am not paying attention (and ADHD is my middle name), her crime goes unnoticed. I often find it has rained while I was at work.

Other times, she is more impishly overt, like when she poured her water on our new beagle puppy sleeping at her feet. She laughed and laughed. Sometimes, the best jokes are strictly for one's own amusement.

It is all fair game and all who choose to play are rewarded with connection, affection, and retaliation. This week, Elijah was riding in the car and began to drink from a water bottle he assumed was mine. I said, "Actually that is Barb's." Elijah, with an immediate wit, victorious smile, dramatically wiped off the mouth saying, "I don't want to get autism." Their fun, non-pity jabs go way back. When he was almost three, we were driving to a water park near St. George Island. Barb was sitting next to Elijah, who was secured like a rhesus monkey astronaut in his trusty car seat. E asked rhetorically just for confirmation joy, "Are we going to the water park?" Barb, whose accurate verbal phrases can only be summoned with pronounced effort and formidable concentration, commanded, "You are not going!" He cried and cried until I could assure him differently and conveyed that Barb was just joking. Barb clapped her hands and laughed for a good five minutes.

When Barb moved next door to us, we had a huge neighborhood block party complete with live band, Heineken keg, Olympic games, swimming, great food, house blessing with real clergy, and a comedy roast. Armed with a captive wrap around porch audience due to a summer shower and an excellent PA system, I hosted the Barb roast. It was shooting fish in a barrel: old money, half-blind, autistic, virgin, mute… could this get any better? Everyone had a blast. At the house blessing, I cried like a premenstrual woman eating Clomid with wine spritzer chasers during a "feed the children" commercial. Love was summoned and pervaded her new home, flowing through all those generous friends, family, and neighbors. What a glorious day to be alive to share so much with those you love.

By lightening up and connecting, we can all help those with ASD become less alone so they, too, may contribute and take ownership in community.

I intend to have Barb' back as we age. When her parents can no longer be there for her...I will.

Please take a moment to think about your friends.

My turn.

I have always been blessed with excellent friends. My oldest, best friend is Gina. She is a successful gynecologist in Memphis, Tennessee, who developed an "aesthetics" division of her practice. Gina has always been smarter, richer, thinner, better dressed, and prettier than me. We met in high school when her eyebrows were bushier and moved with her facial expressions. Gina is a brainy introvert and our friendship began in some lame economics class where she promptly earned her first "U" in conduct. ("U" = unsatisfactory). Or was it an "N" for needs improvement? No matter. Gina was mortified. It took years, but I finally convinced her to let it go, as laughing and connecting is almost always worth the price. Conduct grades never concerned me as my plan ever since grammar school was to have maximum fun socially while still earning good grades and an eventual college scholarship. My plan worked. Now, I notice our son must have similar intent. I use my best psychology to show empathy and active listening when his grave-faced teachers present the serious matter of his clowning.

Although she looks a good ten years younger than me now, Gina is actually a year older (I think its that darn yoga that I refuse to do because I am not sure how one wins.). Anyway, old Gina earned her academic scholarship to a fine private college first. So, granting myself permission to be excused from some string of high school senior classes I deemed not vital to my path, I showed up at her dorm room bearing frozen yogurt. She has always been a health nut with a sweet tooth. Shy Gina was pleased with the offering and didn't protest when I let her know that we would be roommates in the fall.

We were a great team. Through college and graduate schools, Gina grounded me and helped me obey enough rules to be able to continue in the systems. Barely. My "ask forgiveness not permission policy" (which still fuels many of my endeavors) almost got me kicked out of college and grad school. Fortunately, I listened to her sound logic enough to stay in the game. In turn, I assisted her socially. She heeded my advice that a head nod with the briefest of eye contact was not a sufficient greeting for nonstrangers. Gina is a quick study in all things, and we simply role-played and practiced how not to be perceived as a snob.

These days, Gina has droves of friends and a large happy, brilliant family. Gina would have me note "large" as in "many"—three, an acceptable Catholic family procreation number—not "large" in the way that gets Michelle Obama in a tizzy, and I run a respectable company and (usually) think things through with more patience and foresight. We remain close and our children are like cousins and our spouses are dear friends. We are sisters who shared our strengths and are both better off.

Years later, Sister Barb came along. "Sister Barb" is one of her favorite aliases. You see, her Mother is also named Barbara (It is a proud Mayflower descendant kinda thing; whereas my people were happy to limbo the Ellis Island turnstiles fast enough to be called whatever got them a coal mining gig putting our short, sturdy, bowlegged selves to quick use.). To differentiate some mailings and add a little Catholic humor, Barb dons the "Sister" title. She justifies, "I have gone without sex and talking long enough to be grandfathered in, but am not Catholic enough to feel guilty about this black and white collar crime." As an autistic mute, Barb trumped even Gina's introversion and social awkwardness. It was clearly time for more strength sharing on an even larger scale.

Barb and I share strengths. Her Mule and Muse analogy in the next chapter 13, is a reasonable accounting of the commodities exchanged. We are both better off.

Please take a moment to consider someone with Autism who may have not yet had the opportunity for strength sharing in friendship. As you picture them in your mind, you may consider feeling sorry for them. Don't. Pity serves no one. Now, you may feel uncertain how to help. The trap is thinking that the solution to this problem lies outside of you.

Be still. Feel what your life would be like without friends.

Nietzsche said, "He who has a why to live can bear almost any how." Many with Autism are stoically living with a hellacious "How." What if we open our hearts and connect—without words if necessary? Give them the sweet gift of "why"—because we are friends.

To begin a friendship with a person who struggles with Autism, it is helpful to release your pride in having the strengths of language and navigation ease in society. Later, you may realize how prosaic your strengths are by comparison. Clock out of the active lifestyle and just be. Simply exist concomitantly. It is enough. Refreshing, actually. One may wish to start by joining them in a preferred activity. Barb and I like to sit together on the wooden bench swing in her yard. We do not speak at this time. (Okay, Barb does, but it is usually that same old—same old about the mail-truck.) We just listen to each other and our surroundings. Rushing is counter-productive to such quality time. If your busy mind is not yet practiced at just being with another person, perhaps sending direct thoughts of love and blessing will give you something to do as you gain experience in connecting. Don't try to communicate, help, or God forbid …teach—just share time and space. As joy and relaxation are exchanged, you, too, will receive strengths.

The friendship may take time and selfless goodwill to materialize. As Tim Sanders writes in *Love is the Killer App*, "The difference is significant like Ham and Eggs. The chicken is involved but the pig is committed." Be committed. Become significant. You will both be better off.

How wonderful it is that nobody need wait a single moment before starting to improve the world. ~Anne Frank

Our annual Thanksgiving. Top row: John, Annette, Elijah, Aidan, Blake, David, Ryan, Pat, Wilma, Julie, Sara, Christina, and Ty. Top step: Freida, Robin, Brody, and Mandi. Middle step: Linda, Patty, Shaun, Jeff, and Joy. Bottom row: Lois, Barb, Hazel, Charles, and Rachel.

Chapter 13

The Meaning of Life: Child's Play

"Creating a new theory is not like destroying an old barn and erecting a skyscraper in its place. It is rather like climbing a mountain and gaining new and wider views." Albert Einstein

I'm a contemplative. Before that, you may have known me as ADHD, ODD, MR, PDD, ASD, and Brat. Diagnosis change so it is wise not to teach to the diagnosis but to the person. Dominance has a way of creating injustice. The plodding progress of civil rights teaches us that the majority does not respect the rights of the minority until all other options are unpalatable. Please consider this package prejudice perspective as we seek to teach those who are not from the dominant human tribe of neurotypicals.

Being a contemplative means I spend most of my time thinking about things that are not present and observing that which is. It is a tidy job, but somebody has to do it. My "severe autism" makes me more equipped than most for this calling. You splendid children with Autism know what I mean.

Children with ASD special abilities are my audience for this chapter, because I seek to present a meaning of life from a perspective I think we share. In *Constructing Autism: Unraveling the "Truth" and Understanding the Social*, Maji Holmer Nadesan sites Hans Asperger's 1991 article on "autistic strengths," specifically his comments on his patient's "originality of experience" meaning, "Autistic children have the ability to see things and events around them from a new point of view, which often shows surprising maturity" (I think his use of the word 'maturity' is unfortunate, but you get the gist. Our unique talents make knowing direct.).

Our neurotypical siblings almost always seek beyond the answers and then must double back. As in the movie, *Jaws*, the shark is chomping up bathers right off the shore, yet the crusading heroes take the hunt way out to sea. Dramatic, but not efficient.

Scurrying about way out is not how to see. Being there is.

Children, all children, know the meaning of life is closer. It is here. We have it. We are aware. We appreciate the colors in a water drop, our hair follicles warming and expanding in the sun, the slick coolness of a shaded blade of grass, and the tingling of our flesh as sound waves dance off. We notice. We listen in the now. As they grow older, neurotypical folk seem to lose that or rather trade away this innate bounty in some coming of age deal. Shame.

Walkie-talkie diagnosticians often proclaim we ASD folk are in "our own world." Indeed, we are. It is the world of the moment. They were not kicked out of our Eden, but rather ate the apple of action and traveled to a busy state.

William Johnston, in his edition of *The Cloud of Unknowing and the Book of Privy Counseling* presents a clear view of the difference between the contemplative and active life by relating to the Biblical story of the two sisters, Mary and Martha. Luke 10:38-42 reads, "Now as they went on their way, he entered a certain village, where a woman named Martha welcomed him into her home. She has a sister named Mary, who sat at the Lord's feet and listened to what he was saying. But Martha was distracted by her many tasks; so she came to him and asked, "Lord, do you not care that my sister has left me to do all the work by myself? Tell her then to help me." But the Lord answered her, "Martha, Martha, you are worried and distracted by many things; there is need only of one thing.

Mary has chosen the better part, which will not be taken away from her."

Mary listens while Martha labors. Sound familiar? I can't remember the last time I labored, but listen…well, it is our nature. Martha represents the active way of life. Here, Mary represents the contemplative.

Jesus states that, "Mary has chosen the better part." That part is often what we auts do so well.

Jacques's monologue in Shakespeare's play, *As You Like It*, is

All the world's a stage,
And all the men and women merely players;
They have their exits and their entrances;
And one man in his time plays many parts,
His acts being seven ages.

Know your part. Be your part. Play your part with pride and conviction.
Hold your head up and project your voice.

Parker Palmer in *To Know as We Are Known*, explains it beautifully, "We build a world by the sweat of what lies behind our brows."

Any play is infinitely more interesting and profound with rich, diverse characters like ourselves. However, if one can merge the two ways of being, then you have really harnessed power of biblical proportions. Consider the brilliant quantum physicists, Dr. Stephen Hawking. Due to a neuromuscular disease, he can no longer speak and is almost completely paralyzed. His "disability" also makes contemplation his primary way of life. He is an outstanding thinker who has changed the knowledge of the world, but if it were not for a cadre of active lifers funded by grants and goodwill for his

24/7 care and state of the art communication system, his recondite contemplations would be another tree falling in the woods for no one to hear.

Here's a direct quote from Dr. Hawking's website:

For a time, the only way I could communicate was to spell out words letter by letter, by raising my eyebrows when someone pointed to the right letter on a spelling card. It is pretty difficult to carry on a conversation like that, let alone write a scientific paper. However, a computer expert in California, called Walt Woltosz, heard of my plight. He sent me a computer program he had written, called Equalizer. This allowed me to select words from a series of menus on the screen by pressing a switch in my hand. The program could also be controlled by a switch, operated by head or eye movement. When I have built up what I want to say, I can send it to a speech synthesizer. At first, I just ran the Equalizer program on a desktop computer. However, David Mason, of Cambridge Adaptive Communication, fitted a small portable computer and a speech synthesizer to my wheelchair. This system allowed me to communicate much better than I could before. I can manage up to fifteen words a minute. I can either speak what I have written, or save it to disk. I can then print it out, or call it back and speak it sentence by sentence. Using this system, I have written a book and dozens of scientific papers. I have also given many scientific and popular talks. They have all been well received.

> *I think that is in a large part due to the quality of the speech synthesizer, which is made by Speech Plus. One's voice is very important. If you have a slurred voice, people are likely to treat you as mentally deficient: Does he take sugar? This synthesizer is by far the best I have heard, because it varies the intonation, and doesn't speak like a Dalek. The only trouble is that it gives me an American accent.*

I know how he feels. My go-to voice is SS reading aloud what I type. I tried computer-generated voices but prefer hers as she understands my sentiments and has my timing down pat, but Lordy, her Southern twang, is disconcerting. My own voice is of course more elegant but it is still in the shop.

Allow me to introduce an excerpt from an upcoming children's book where I portray a coming together of an active and a contemplative life.

The Mule and the Muse
In Smiling Nelda

During one particularly amusing time/space particle arrangement, there lived a beautiful, fair-haired muse who was well versed in the communication shortcuts the universal system had to offer. Gladness, the muse's given name, would spend her days flitting about this dimension and that voicelessly whispering to peasants, warriors, highly evolved nonhuman species, toads, infants of every kind, and to any being that tickled her dainty nose with interest.

One day while loafing about her own history, Gladness was tugged toward the eyes of a sturdy mule.

The muse was intrigued as she was now the recipient of the mule's inspiring whisper.

Gladness eventually named her burly peer. This was primarily for the purpose of attributing ownership to various thoughts they synergized. These friends thought ownership was not used to foster pride but to help one better know the workings and style of the other's mind. Mule's label was Daisy. The muse spontaneously created this title one bleak, winter dusk and implemented it immediately. Good-natured Daisy made no protest and was rather pleased since yellow was her favorite color. Gladness was confident she made the right choice, as daisies are friends to all children and quite literally down to earth.

A big part of their communication usually involved planning how to make the muse's existence more full of productive purpose.

Daisy was already a solid contributor to the universal good. But the muse had ridden the wind's coattail for long enough. It was time to get a job, one suitable for a muse, of course. Sweat would not be involved.

Gladness fantasized about many grandiose callings. She would be a clever sooth and set up shop on a remote tropical beach planted beneath a 100-year-old palm. Distraught poets who have lost clarity in their inner eyes would seek relief and a creativity jump-start from the unspoken words of the insightful muse. Frustrated athletes would pilgrimage yearning for renewed focus. Soundless musicians would journey for melody and direction. Housewives would clamor to the helpful muse for inspirational family-pleasing dinner recipes, right behind renowned chefs struggling to retain their reputations for novel and exquisite palate sensations. Practical Daisy pointed out the paucity of demands due to logistics and the marketing challenges for such a position. It was agreed that Gladness would pursue writing instead.

It should be noted that by their very nature, muses do not work alone no matter how light the task.

End excerpt.

They need us and we need them. My dear autistic peers we are of value. We are stewards of the meaning of life.

The meaning of life is a gift that can stay with us, comforting and providing like a well-worn knapsack always with our person. This knapsack of knowing each moment can be carelessly left at the train station as so many do at about age ten or eleven when they transition away from being fully present to scampering around in the world of adult baggage.

How many times have we observed children being absorbed in the moment joy of gurgling orange drinks, breathlessly swinging, eating snow, giggling and chasing, splashing, climbing with wide adventurous eyes …only to be bridled away from that purpose in life by an adult. "All right, that's enough, you're going to fall, get me wet, catch your death of cold, choke…and forget the meaning of life."

We each know the meaning of life. We each make the meaning. That is the point of free will.

Some normals understand only after a catastrophe. If they are terminally ill or had a close call, they often are inspired to reclaim their meaning of life lickety-split. Then they smell the roses and cut grass, really taste their manicotti, think inside and laugh outside, caress the frosty condensation on a cold Coke, and purposely sit front row to symphonies of silence.

For those of you who require a more literal scan of the knapsack's contents before you trust it is safe to travel with, I suggest you read Leo Tolstoy's playful classic, *The Three Questions*. The loquacious emperor learns from a taciturn hermit: **The most important time is now, the most important person is the one(s) you are with at this moment, and the most important thing to do is help them be happy. And that, my friends, is the meaning of life.**

My 2,054 words are a simple, "Post-it note" reminder to my young autistic friends. Take the train to maturation, but don't forget your autistic bag.

Practical Implications

1. "You can't change the past. You can't even change the future, in the sense that you can only change the present one moment at a time, stubbornly, until the future unwinds itself into the stories of our lives." (Larry Wall, the inventor of Perl programming language)

2. Saint Bridget reminds us, "We become that which we love." Slow down and recall who you are and what you love. You will find they are one and the same.

3. Free will is the best deal ever. Take it—and enjoy carefully matching your words and actions with your highest self.

Projecting my voice. (Barb typing with back support only.)

Chapter 14

Resource

I recommend praying before every session, appointment, meeting, class, operation…whatever form your day takes. This is no substitute for training and no need for Pharisees pomp and circumstance—just take a moment to make your complete focus be the well being of the other person(s). At the office, I literally go to the bathroom between each session not because I am too cheap for a good pair of Depends, but to wash my hands (…and, for our over analytical audience, not in a Lady Macbeth kinda way). It is hygienic as we see a lot of clients, some of whose preferred stim is nose picking and booger eating (A little guy had one this week that was audibly sandy). Crotch digging is another popular stim for our ASD clients. I also find this to be a consistent opportunity to tidy up the area and put the seat down so none of our Gucci Moms fall in. No one wants private therapy rates and gas station facilities. If you think neurotypical boys are bad about poor aim and seat crimes…try those struggling with ADHD and ASD. That said, the most important thing I do in that 90 seconds—is pray.

Yes. I pray. And it works, too!

"Prayer from the heart can achieve what nothing else can in the world…. Properly understood and applied, it is the most potent instrument of action…." Mahatma Gandhi

I agree with Barb: Buddhist, Hindu, Jewish, Christian, Islamic—whatever the seasoning, the primary ingredient is Source. Servers, let us stand on the shoulders of giants who connected through nonself-serving prayer: Mahatma Gandhi, Dr. Martin Luther King, Nelson Mandela, and the Dalai Lama (hmm, I best think of a nonbrown person who fought for the rights of those whose voices were not being heard lest some of you be offended or not relate…got it, Mother Teresa…okay, tan, but not brown).

Prayer connects us. Barb and I are here to share that we find CONNECTION is the best "treatment" for Autism. Find opportunities to connect. Prayer is one way.

Snow Claire and our beloved Claire (1997 – 2011)
teaching Elijah and me impermanence.

Chapter 15

Barb Day

"Who are you Jesus in the Temple?"

These are the words uttered by my dear, frenzied smiling shrink (SS) as she and a handsome Boston PD officer scurried up to me and my new bar pals. I was sitting and drinking a frosty coke and having the most delightful, lighthearted conversation with these laughing ladies. Normally, such an exchange does not bring down the law, but with me, there is always a twist. Allow me to retrace my shoeless steps.

The day was going well. Today was to be the crescendo of the last two weeks. At 1:30 pm, I was scheduled to present excerpts from our book, along with my take on facilitated communication (FC).

I tailored the day for maximum relaxation and concentration. I slumbered until my dreams were complete and my eager, beady eyes popped open. My perpetually moving SS was humming about the hotel room taking care of this and that so when I awakened, I need only point my way to any number of happy options. I was instantly handed a cold Coke and sparklingly clean eyeglasses before my sleepy feet were even required to hit the floor—as I have come to expect in utopia.

You see, this week unlike all others in my thirty years, I was waited on hand and foot by my traveling mate with whom I am able to type fluently. To be able to express more than a "yes" or "no" throughout my day and have her perky disposition dispensing undivided 24/7 attention was remarkable. I was taking full advantage of this twist of fate.

This is about as good as it gets in my book. I felt like Elvis. Had I requested to have old gospel tunes piped into my suite and dine every thirty minutes on fried peanut butter and banana sandwiches, it would surely have been arranged. So, we were off for a brief swim, which relaxes me more than eight or ten of the King's best Valium. Upon returning to our suite, SS quickly ran me a warm bath so there would be no waiting time for the princess to chill after swim suit disrobing. Please, believe me, I do not demand pampering in life, but am no fool—when it occurs, I notice and wallow in it.

I am quickly scrubbed clean, clean, clean and as instructed, SS started the timer on my fifteen-minute uninterrupted soak. This day, I throw in a request to listen to a fabulous audio book, *Mutant Messenger/Down Under*. It is an extraordinary tale about a fifty-year-old physician who is treated to remember the secrets of the universe by a small tribe of in tune Aborigines. Yes, the good doctor got the whole scoop from telepathy to mental healing and oneness. This is a must read, but I digress. Next, I am dressed, but not in my favorite outfit I previously selected to wear during my upcoming presentation. Oh, no, my attendant is far too savvy for that. For my more than slightly messy, in room dining experience, I wear velvet warm ups for my comfort and dining efficiency. Hugh Hefner would surly recruit my gal, Friday, had he known about her ascot wielding comprehensive commitment. The incessant, vexatious humming could be negotiated out at a future time.

After devouring our tasty luncheon, I am given time for a leisurely BM. Again, I take full advantage of the services and am soon fighting weight as I dress for the presentation. We arrive on time and all smiles.

The talk went extremely well. My work had the normals laughing, crying, and asking lil ol me many follow-up questions and serious advice. I have never, never felt of more value. Giving the best I had to grateful souls had me feeling on top of the universe.

After the presentation, Tom Page and I shared an unprecedented conversation for all the world to see. We typed to each other. Tom is a prominent member of the Special Forces and is an eloquent and loquacious user of telepathy. He and I have voicelessly chatted many times before. It was good to put a face with a mind.

Finally, it was time to return to our room and have me mentally refuel. That was what SS was thinking. This clever nut had other plans. I intended to ride this competency wave to the shore... let the good times roll.

SS has precious little fuel reserves, so I knew I could parlay her inevitable hunger into the opportunity of a lifetime. Bingo. She didn't last thirty minutes. She asked me if I wanted a snack from the healthy bakery/fresh fruit stand in the mall attached to our hotel. It was all I could do to guard my mischievous mental plans from my kind victim as I typed. But where there is a will there is a fraudulent way. I typed, "Not hungry. I would like to wind down here and watch *CNN*. Go without me. I will be fine right here in my king-size refueling station. Go."

After a few double checks, I simply hit 'yes' on the board to assure her my intent to vegetate. Finally, she left. But not without conducting the most banal security exercise. The little shit walked all the way to the elevator then stealthily returned to room 912, put her fluffy hairs against the door, and listened.

I froze. Who does she think she is dealing with? She knows I can hear loud sounds like her clunky shoes on carpet and floppy brunette locks banging on our metal door. But, I was relieved when she eventually turned away and skipped toward the elevators since explaining why I was up with my best spectacles on and picking up my purse from across the room would have been difficult and probably raised too many suspicions for my current plan to be implemented.

There was no time to spare. I considered my sock feet condition and knew that would be my Achilles heel. Everybody knows only the mentally loose travel about in public with no shoes.

I had no option. Even in my most acute state of competency, I might—might be able to cajole my evil stepsister feet into my shoes, but tying was impossible and laces dragging would surely prove perilous. I must simply rely on the fact that my cozy socks were dark and hopefully no authorities would notice. I was off.

I calculated a ten-minute escape window—tops. SS moves like a gazelle on crack and I more similar to a luded up, arthritic hippo with nearsighted specs left in her other purse.

My destination and goal were clear: lively watering hole and fun conversation with any person willing and able to FC with me. The odds were good that I could find such a gem at this conference since it was for such uniquely designed folk.

My only real obstacle was the elevators. Would I be able to make my ornery appendages strike the "L" with enough accuracy to make a successful descent? No need. Lady luck rode down with me as a portly tourist rhetorically asked, "Lobby?" as he officiously pushed the L.

I then scanned the area for shinny brass. I picked up the glare and was on my way to the bar.

As I envisioned, I had little trouble perusing the minds of the bar patrons and quickly found a happy soul who has a daughter with whom she facilitates. I approached my mark.

I was even able to initiate a breathy, "Hi," which I have been working on in speech therapy for the past few months. And I grinned like a two-year-old running aimlessly in free play. This socially inviting facial expression was also no easy feat. For months, I have been training my face and mouth muscles in speech therapy to make such a well-timed statement. I am on a roll. Ms. Mark invites me to join their boisterous table.

Now, lets not kid anyone here these chatty southern bells pegged me as a Special Forces member, but just not as an escapee. Thank God for dark taverns and matching socks.

I immediately reached in my purse...a convincing move since the sane are usually accessorized. I pulled out a laminated piece of paper, which reads: "Please see my laminated answer for all that ails ya. The time has come for me to by my synergic self and not give thought effort to trying to convince other of my abilities. The questions will always be asked. I need to think of a clever but not defensive response to let the curious and hurtful nonbelievers alike know that my family and I have addressed the authorship issue already too many times to recall. I will no longer be using my precious supported typing times to help others believe in me. If people like my work and I touch lives, then I am contented. I will not be liked by, believed by, or touch everyone. This is true for all thinkers. I am no exception. BarbR"

I could hardly believe my good fortune. I wrote that thing six months ago. Who knew it would be my passport to my first totally unsupervised bar experience?

The buzzing ladies read it aloud and understood immediately. Hell, now they even knew my name. And smooth Barb then handed them my laminated letter board from deep in my purse. As I write this account, it occurs to me that I couldn't perform such a detailed task today if I were prompted to grab and keep a $100,000 bill from that damn purse. But that day—the amazing Barb surfed gracefully in the world of tipsy normals.

Today was Barb's Day. The facilitating mom offered me her small boned, creamy soft hand and away we went. I was quickly offered the drink of my choosing. I paused. My first preference would probably not be wise. I desired a Guinness, room temperature. I decided not to press my luck with even the slightest cognitive impairment. I typed, "Coke, please." It arrived instantaneously. These chosen hostesses were very hospitable and even presented me with bowl after bowl of bar snacks. We exchanged the usual "Where are you from?" tidbits and even some less than regular barroom diddies about autism and my typing hand preference. The crazy thing is I am almost always able to type only with my dominant left hand. But today, I was so mentally and physically efficient that my right hand navigated the board with the support of her dainty hand as I stuffed my face with peanuts, pretzels, and frosty coke sips with my left! My feet were still available and I considered juggling long necks but figured my sock feet would provide too much negative press.

Time passed quickly for me, but not so for SS who had to relinquish her moniker for that hour and a half and even began to cry a bit. She made the logical rounds immediately after searching under the bed, in the closet, behind the curtains, and around the shower.

Some of the sections of this tale I gleamed from SS's firsthand account to me after we reconnected. But much of it I got while piggybacking in her mind and looking out her rapidly darting eyes. I was a machine. Yes, I can read minds and communicate telepathically, but I have never attempted such a taxing feat while typing and acting damn near normal.

I viewed her maturely calling hotel security within the first twenty seconds of the discovery. Her voice was serious but calm and commanding. The emergency lady was doing SS's biddings without hesitation. All hotel security was dispatched immediately. Clever SS also made sure the connecting mall forces were on the job, too. All exits were secure. Her description of me was unsettlingly exact. She even stressed the shoeless point.

Two minutes into my vacation, three hotel security officers, forty mall police, and one highly focused SS was on the trail of the vulnerable, nonverbal me. I would have preferred the posse stop there. But, the sagacious SS was pulling out all stops and being a pretty attractive extrovert served her well.

I seriously considered calling the whole thing off with some type of ludicrous attention-drawing behavior when I witnessed her stopping a play in progress performed by Special Forces members in front of an audience packed with hundreds of well meaning conference goers. She got the microphone and without a second thought began her urbane plea for assistance. Her words clogged in her throat like insanely lumpy oatmeal. Her eyes burned hot then filled but not to the dripping point with acidic tears. I think it was a guilt/real fear combo. At any rate, those concerned for my well-being and quick recovery grew exponentially.

The gig would be up soon. I will be as charming as possible in the meantime. But damn, I was mentally busy.

You see I had a dual purpose for my excursion. In addition to generating significant adventure and good story material, I wanted to test SS's mental reception and faith skills. Could she find me with her rusty tools?

My experiment was confounded because the tools at her immediate disposal were sharp, quick, and she implemented them expertly. Damn it, she may find me with those assets before I had a chance to make her rely on the esoteric truths just reviewed in *Mutant Messenger*.

Her brain activity was so loud, I was starting to fear she would be unable to hear my calls. But least we forget today is "Barb's day" and all the planets have aligned in reverent homage.

My opportunity soon emerged, but only after one more over the top recon resource was ignited. SS got on the phone to the Boston police department and put out a formal 911 missing person's deal.

Oh, boy, my day was getting expensive. The good news was she was required to stand quietly in the lobby and await the gun-toting saviors. She did and her brain rested. Ring, ring Barb calling....

About an hour into my elopement, my frazzled, guilt ridden do-gooder began to figure it out. I was sending clues as fast and as powerfully as my neurons could fire. "Put the rock in your mouth, put the rock in your mouth...," I unceasingly sent this mantra. What fun! I shamelessly stole this reference from the *Mutant Messenger* book. I know it is not original, but the faith-based action message should have been clear to SS since I knew she heard all of that book.

My intent was to have her become me mentally and thus find me through my own mind's eye.

I know, I know, I really should get out more, but we all have our hobbies. Anyway, she was piecing it together. Actually, she was about to take a cop out road and tried to call Tom, the telepath, to ask him to type where I was. Oh, but least you think SS is advanced when I say "call,"—I mean the practical gal picked up the phone and tried to call his room. The novice could not be expected to know that no way would Tom lend his services since as soon as Tom visited my mind, he would immediately comprehend the training mission and not interfere with SS's learning and self discovery.

Fortunately, SS was unable to reach good Tom by phone. This bought me a few more minutes. I sent, "Be Barb." "Be Barb." I thought it wise to try a more succinct and remedial message than the previous for my reluctant pupil. She began to take ownership of the message and was clearly heard to turn it around to a first person command. "I am Barb" *I am Barb SS thought.* Now we were getting somewhere.

At that moment she grinned but not without those burning eyes lingering from her overstimulated emotional system. She was beginning to see.

Aha. SS's mind swirled with these understandings: "Barb is with people...a group...a merry group. Barb is okay—more than okay She is not afraid. She is happy. I will see her very soon and will feel relief and love but no anger and disappointment."

I know that is anticlimactic but that is truly how my tale ends. A couple of minutes prior to that limited revelation, SS sent one of the volunteer conference posse to check the bar for anyone who knew Tom Page's whereabouts or phone number. That is when the recruited senior citizen nark spied me and went tattling to the lobby as fast as her remaining bone density would allow.

SS arrived with the most beautiful civil servant a girl could ever wish for. I immediately typed with the soft hand, "I think someone here is in big trouble." True to her mental word, SS was not angry.

She was relieved and happy to see me. After her pithy Jesus reference, she kissed me, thanked my smiling accomplices, and hugged and kissed the hunky Boston PD officer. Obviously, the latter was done just because she can.

The only repercussions were that I was asked to leave my cozy tavern and accompany SS to all remaining conference gatherings to show that we were reunited and that Lois had not killed me with neglect. All posses were notified. Unfortunately, Boston taxpayers picked up the brunt of the tab for Barb Day. Fortunately, for that same tax base, all pleas to the hill lobbying for an annual Barb Day have so far gone unacknowledged.

Practical Implications

1. Swimming = an autistic must.

2. Slid on shoes = see above

3. Open = If you truly want to know an autistic person better...open your mind, be still, and politely ask. Rinse and repeat.

4. Humor = Can be abundantly harvested more often than many think. The richest humor farmers do not take themselves too seriously. I recommend that. Enjoy.

Me and my dear old friend Pat (pun intended – the man is 92) shown joyously sharing mind space on the big screen at one of my presentations.

Chapter 16
Practical Implications to Follow "Barb Day"

The wise are open to learning. Not so open that our brains fall out, but tuned in to gaining knowledge by considering other approaches, perspectives, and possibilities.

In her book, *Constructing Autism: Unraveling the 'Truth' and Understanding the Social*, Majia Nadesan reminds us that society has come along way from locking up the different in ships that sailed without destination or constructing "the great confinement" where madhouse directors bound their inmates in chains and misery. Anyone still game for "mother blaming" the autism epidemic or prescribing opium, cocaine, or cannabis to clear it all up? Trepanning? Leeches? Burning at the stake? No? Precisely. We need not pretend all best practices have been divined and implemented.

Meta-analysis is a statistically intensive methodology used for examining collections of experiments. It is a sound research tool used often in ecology, psychology, sociology, and medicine, which leads to many evidence-based treatments and medicine. I conducted a meta-analysis to complete a Masters of Science degree. Dean Radin, author of *Entangled Minds: Extrasensory Experiences in a Quantum Reality* cites numerous meta-analytic studies in professionally rigorous journals reporting replicable findings of significant effects regarding telepathy.

Radin illuminates the value of being open to perspectives by quoting Richard Feynman's (Nobel Laureate and world-famous quantum physicist) reaction to Thomas Young's frequently replicated double-slit experiment. This experiment yields a phenomenon involving photons behaving as both

particles and waves. With one slit open, photons shot at a
screen move through and land as particles as common sense
would predict. But when both slits are open, each photon is
found to individually go through both slits at the same time
behaving as a wave and in that state it "interfered or entangled
with itself." Impossible? Maybe. Observed? Yes.

> Feynman said, "What I am going to tell you is what we
> teach our physics students in the third or fourth year of
> graduate school.... It is my task to convince you not to
> turn away because you don't understand it. You see, my
> physics students don't understand it.... That is because
> I don't understand it. Nobody does."

As controlled lab tests teach us more about interconnected,
entangled physical reality, an increasing number of scientists
are challenging conventional perspectives about what is
possible. Albert Einstein wrote the preface to Pulitzer Prize-
winning author, Upton Sinclair's, *Mental Radio* where Sinclair
describes that his wife could reproduce sketches that he drew
sitting many miles away and other findings of mental
connectivity. Einstein's thoughts of telepathy are expressed in
a conversation with another theoretical physicist in P.A.
Schilipp's *Albert Einstein: Philosopher-Scientists*, "He: I am
inclined to believe in telepathy. Einstein: This has probably
more to do with physics than with psychology."

To the question, "Is telepathy real?" I offer, "I don't
know." But, I believe sober arguments and data support such
research worthy of consideration. Ernest Rutherford, known as
"the father of nuclear physics" famously states, "All of physics
is either impossible or trivial. It is impossible until you
understand it and then it becomes trivial."

To the question, "Have you observed Barb to communicate telepathically? I offer a more parsimonious answer, "Yes. I think so."

It is interesting to note the 2003 findings from the Institute of Noetic Sciences that compile a profile for people who are most likely to present psychic abilities: "a left-handed female who is thirty something or younger, physically highly sensitive, suffers from chronic anxiety, is somewhat introverted, makes decisions based more on feeling than logic, practices one or more creative arts, engages in some form of mental discipline like mediation, is open to unconventional claims, and is interested more in possibilities than facts."

The only thing they left out was Barb's height and weight.

Sometimes, it is wise to be open to nonconventional thinking. I had dinner with a friend, KL, visiting from London and she shared the following account. Please note she is a mathematically minded, fact-driven realist who is a military intelligence specialist. KL shares precious few of the aforementioned traits associated with those who experience extra sensory phenomenon.

KL's Army job usually has her poring over a computer twelve hours a day digesting intelligence data from myriad sources to try and discern patterns and foresee movements and threats. But this day, her superiors assigned her to patrolling the Iraqi streets to compliment her training with real time, field perspectives. The night before this mission, KL could not sleep. She was worried. KL has participated in numerous off base assignments and is a confident solider. This was different. She could not put her finger on the dread, but mental whispers of "sniper trouble" persisted, although the chatter and intel to which she is directly privy forecasted "all clear."

The morning of the drive, reports revealed that sniper activity was indeed likely. As the three Humvee convoy drove, they encountered a possible explosive device in the road and a removal team was called. As they waited for it to be cleared, the stop began to feel too long. KL shared with her fellow soldiers that "something inside me was saying we had been there too long." The feeling pervaded her mind. Something wasn't right. At that moment, she was asked to go into the hatch and guard.

KL elaborated, "As soon as I came out of the hatch, I got an eerie feeling. There were no longer people walking around or moving about on the streets. Across from our position was a tall mill building, perfect for a sniper. I kept my eye on that tower."

Her insight, intuition, whatever it was—became actionable intelligence and she immediately kept her head and torso moving as if someone were watching her as a possible target.

After a few minutes, a shadow moved atop the mill. Some doves flew up and another crewmember also saw the movement. Game on. In what seemed like "no time" she learned by feeling it as tangible as a breeze—"the look" moved from her to the guard perch in the second Humvee.

A single shot rang out. The radio relayed panic as that solider was shot in the neck. He died.

KL lives because she was open to learning through unorthodox knowing.

Your unconscious brain may be better at processing information than your conscious mind. Psychologists call this adaptive unconscious. This burgeoning field of study examines rapid decision-making, which produces judgments and behaviors before the individual recognizes that conclusions have been made.

Malcolm Gladwell popularizes the phenomena of adaptive unconscious in his book, *Blink*. He argues that although unconscious processes occur automatically and without our awareness, that through concerted effort and practice and we can learn to control even implicit aspects of the self.

Barb is all about exercising her mind. Perhaps our adaptive unconscious can link up? Such connections would be evolutionarily efficient.

*Cave entrance where Ty and I had our first date and experience
with spelunking. That day our geographer buddy chiseled through a
wall as he suspected another passage to follow. It did! He was too
large to enter, but Ty and I crawled in to discover a waterfall never before
seen by humans. Sometimes the tiny roads less traveled are
just too interesting not to explore.*

Chapter 17

Parents/Source—The Gift of Being Part of the Solution

How any of us gather strength and support is basically the same—we tap into the Source. In fact, I am doing it right now. People give many names and structures to Source. But labels don't matter. The Source is the Source is the Source. The Source is all that matters. That which is not matter is Source, too.

We heal and strengthen by ceasing to be dualistic with our perceptions of self. **When we remember who we are as flecks of God, shavings of Source, some of the Sum, whatever you wish to call it, we accept the perpetual gift of being part of the solution**. The Buddhist proverb, "When the student is ready, the teacher will appear" is true. The Source always provides the gift when we are ready to accept.

President Lincoln accepted this gift, my parents accepted this gift, and finally, so did I. **Everyone's path is different, but everyone's solution is the same—Source.**

President Lincoln was a logical thinker who did not respect those who thought they were religiously for sure correct. Honest Abe was no fan of pious blowhards who thought they had all the answers. Author Evans Roth shares this sentiment in *Brains, Religions, and Reality: Integrative Searching for Purpose and Peace*, "Science will always be incomplete, by definition. Too often, religious leaders seem to act as though religion is complete."

God in America: "A Nation Reborn" (PBS series #3) outlines how Lincoln tapped into the Source and fulfilled his destiny. In Lincoln's first inauguration, he proposed a compromise. Southerners rejected his plea as they felt the Bible clearly protected and prescribed the right to own slaves. The North also felt the Lord was on their side. Both sides believed God favored their cause. **Not remembering "I might be you" and we are all of Source —off to war they went.**

The war raged on and was beyond brutal. Lincoln toured hospitals and sat with the wounded. He bemoaned, "If Hell is not any worse than this, it has no terror for me." Lincoln's heart changed when his third and favorite son, Willie, died at the age of eleven from typhoid fever. The eulogy impelled him to consider trusting in a loving God. Abraham's reexamination of his relationship with Source, lead to his noetic truth, "The will of God prevails." From there, Lincoln took the gift of being part of the solution and turned to the plight of our war-torn country and agonized over, "What is the will of God in this crisis?" He knew both sides maybe wrong, but one must be wrong. Lincoln discerned that God cannot be for both and against the same thing at the same time (This was years before wave-particle duality of light was known, so we will cut Abe some slack.). He reasoned, therefore, that God must will this conflict. Lincoln's role then was to lead in such a way that good could come from this war.

My Dear Dad (DD) went through a parallel process when his third child and favorite daughter, Barb, died at the age of two and a half from Autism. DD accepted his role to lead in such a way that good could come from this ASD war.

"If we are right," says Lincoln, "and if what we are doing is good in the sight of God, then we have to carry it through to its fruition because in the process of making African-Americans free, we are freeing ourselves. And once we free ourselves, then we can begin again." If one would please reread the above quote and insert "Barb" in place of "African-Americans," one will begin to understand my parent's resolve concerning our Autistic wars.

Lincoln found comfort in the story of Job (And who doesn't? What a fun read.). My DD is a big Job fan, too. Like President Lincoln, President Rentenbach took his Job job to heart and task. These men set out to fix our world in the direction that God wills. Dad is a man who always owns being part of the solution.

DD went about solving the crisis of me being enslaved in Autism first with logic and then with faith and a clear sense of God's will.

I valorize both Presidents Lincoln and Rentenbach as their determination lead to evolution. **When enough of us embrace being part of the solution, eventually, justice prevails and discrimination bails.**

Mom's role in ameliorating our autistic problem was also vital. She is less diplomatic and presidential and more like a keen, tenacious, and impassioned defense attorney. She was my independence dream team. Her mission was my civil rights and freed speech.

Like Clarence Darrow who represented John Scopes (the young biology teacher who disobeyed the Tennessee ban on teaching evolution in 1925) in the "trial of the century," Mom fought the autistic monkey on my back with science, science, and more science. She took me to every doctor, expert, and intervention program imaginable. Fastidious, lionhearted Mom immersed herself in my care and healing. One of my favorite theologians, Karen Armstrong, writes "ekstasis" is the "stepping outside" of the prism of selfishness. Mom did that.

In the Scopes trial, the question was about who had authority—laws of science or religion? The judge was not impartial and favored the fundamentalist position championed by prosecutor and itinerant preacher, William Jennings Bryan.

Darrow wanted to put scientists (who were Christian) on the stand, but the judge would not allow it. When Darrow hit a dead end with science, he went straight to the source and asked William Jennings Bryan to take the stand as a Bible expert. Bryan's testimony revealed illogical circular reasoning concerning the literal interpretation of the Bible. Darrow was declared a clear winner by the people and press. Bryan's own words were so damning to his case that the biased judge had the testimony removed the next day. Scopes was found guilty but public opinion was on his side. **Ignorance was exposed, but not yet mended. Justice almost always takes more time than the just expect**.

In my case, when Mom hit a dead end with science, she went straight to the source and asked me to take the stand as an Autism expert. We flew up to Syracuse, New York, and had me fitted for words at the Institue for Facilitated Communication. The suit fit. I was ready to testify. Many judges also threw out my testimony. But eventually, enough public opinion favored my rights and I gained freedom.

No longer were "they" treating me. I made my case and cure with my own words.

Happy as a freed slave, I now accept my gift of being part of the solution.

We autistics are often aficionados about systems and patterns. I process details first and then am able to work up to the gestalt. Studying history and philosophy helps me better understand people. Dean Radin in <u>Entangled Minds,</u> writes that I am in good company with this hermeneutic pastime, "H.G. Wells said that history is a race between education and catastrophe. Philosopher George Santayana offered similar advice, warning that those who cannot remember the past are condemned to repeat it."

In Decision Points by George W. Bush, he reflects that the nature of history is that we only know the consequences of our actions but inactions have consequences, too.

My part of the solution is to slow down and take the time to tune in and ferret out good paths and whether they be best trod by action or inaction. Then I am supposed to tell it. Granted, I clocked in late, but I intend to do my job as well as my parents did theirs so that I may be part of the solution for others.

Freud wrote that what is moral is self-evident. It may be self-evident but it is not automatic. And what is intuited to be right is definitely not always followed with solution-oriented action. Did we not feel and thus know slavery was wrong? Disregarding Autistics? Annihilating Jews and homosexuals? Casting down untouchables? Crusading with slaughter? Raping the Earth? Our inconsistencies fill history. Many of us are here to balance the scales by helping us remember "I might be you." It's about jobs. **Some of the Sum, lets get to work.**

Practical Implications:

1. Since justice almost always takes more time than the just expect, one must not procrastinate when accepting the gift of being part of the solution.

2. Make amends.

3. "All the greatest and most important problems of life are fundamentally insolvable. They can never be solved, but only outgrown." (Carl Jung) The good news is human growth is a natural byproduct of education and reflection, both of which can be quite enjoyable.

Jerry and me embracing being part of each other's solution

Chapter 18

Ten Strategies of Successful Parents Who Have Children with Autism

It has been my pleasure to know many extraordinary people who have children with autism. They are wellsprings of approaches and mindsets that equip them for weathering heartbreaks and challenges with grace and stamina. ***These ten strategies are based on the stalwart examples of such parents who successfully manage the chronic stress involved in caring for loved ones with long-term disabilities.***

1. **Document. Legendary management consultant, Peter Drucker, said, "What gets measured, gets managed."** Families who adapt well often keep exceedingly thorough records. In a world where parents may feel overwhelmed and in little control, documenting is helpful and doable. Maintaining well-organized binders chronicling assessments, treatments, therapies, school records, immunization protocols, work products, family photos, and videos of problematic behaviors can provide a wealth of useful information. I encourage practitioners, caregivers, and educators to take the time to read every word. Tony Jeary writes in *Inspire Any Audience*: "No one cares how much you know unless they know how much you care." Not only does taking the time to learn about this person show you care, but it will undoubtedly help you do your job. Such documentation yields practical data from a variety of perspectives about what has been successful and what has not—hopefully inspiring additional ideas about treatment options and improved quality of care.

2. **Optimism**. "You can learn it, you can measure it, you can teach it, and you will be healthier and happier for it" writes prolific research psychologist Martin Seligman in *Learned Optimism: How to Change Your Mind and Your Life*.

    Substantial empirical evidence shows optimists have less mood disturbances in responses to short and long-term stressors. Optimism is also associated with better overall physical health. One plausible explanation is its effects on the immune system. In the *American Psychological Association's 2001* cover story, "A new take on psychoneuroimmunology: Research pointing to a circuit linking the immune system and brain connects illness, stress, mood, and thought in a whole new way," Steven Maier, professor of psychology at the University of Colorado states, we know behavior and psychological events influence the immune system and now we are discovering that there is a loop where the immune system sends signals to the brain, "that potentially alter neural activity and thereby alter everything that flows from neural activity, mainly behavior, thought, and mood." Research shows pessimists get depressed more easily and more often and depression depletes brain hormones creating a chain of biochemical events that slow down the immune system.

    The good news is that a pessimist can learn to be an optimist. Carol Dweck in *Mindset: The New Psychology of Success—How We Can Learn to Fulfill Our Potential* writes that while temperament plays a role, people can be taught "the growth mindset," where they learn to process as optimists who are more likely to take action in response to stressors whereas pessimists may feel defeated making them less likely to take constructive actions. Cognitive Behavior Therapy (CBT), a form of talk therapy that emphasizes the role of thinking on how we feel and what we do, is a good approach to making the mindset change when you are ready.

Henry Ford's advice: "Whether you think you can, or you think you can't—you're right."

3. **Strengths. Build on your Strengths**. Study, meditate, focus, learn, and practice what you do well and enjoy. Read everything you can get your hands on to improve those skill sets. Surround yourself with people who compliment your areas of weakness. A mature person is secure with their identity. You know you are a good parent—heck, if you are like most of our dear clients, you are an outstanding parent. **You cannot be everything to your child—no one can. Being your highest authentic self has meaning and is the best gift you can give.** As Dolly Parton says, "Find out who you are, and do it on purpose."

4. **Mindfulness. Mindfulness is an excellent way to process stress**. It changes emotional reactions, which are often unconscious to a chosen controlled, fully conscious response. With mindfulness, one can choose to only get angry on purpose and other fun tricks. Suppressing emotions is proven to decrease mental and physical well-being. Specifically holding anger and resentment is counterproductive to good health. But mindfulness allows one to feel and validate emotions and then move on. Sylvia Boorstein in her book, *It's Easier Than You Think*, makes her case that pain is inevitable but suffering is optional. The key is to own the emotion, and then do with it as you will.

Jon Kabat—Zinn shares many practical exercises to develop mindfulness in eating, walking, and breathing in his book, *Full Catastrophe Living: Using the Wisdom of Your Body and Mind to Face Stress, Pain, and Illness.*

Such practice can prepare you well for dealing with outbursts, tantrums, and fits of aggression. Last week, a mostly non-verbal adolescent male with autism became very frustrated with a challenging computer assignment and felt an overwhelming surge of anger. He began hitting the computer. I removed the expensive laptop quickly so he lashed out at the table, desk, lamp, and windows in my office. To help him deescalate promptly, I said, "Wow, you just changed the energy of the room. I felt that anger and tension, too—like an electric jolt. Take a second to notice how anger makes your body feel. It makes my neck tense, face hot, and heart race. After feeling that, I am going to let it go and change my energy back to calm and confident." I did and so did he. Daniel Siegel in *Mindsight: The New Science of Personal Transformation* refers to this type of focused attention as "naming and taming". We were able to finish the session with a noncomputer activity. He knows he will have a chance to work maturely with the computer next week, but the opportunity is gone for now. He felt disappointed and we acknowledged that too. He chose to cry for a moment. Then he put the lamp back up and shook my hand as he left. These steps were successful because he and I have a foundation of shared respect and experience practicing mindfulness exercises. With exposure and practice, your children will mirror your mindfulness and control.

"What lies behind us and what lies before us are tiny matters compared to what lies within us." Ralph Waldo Emerson

5. **Forgiveness. Resilient parents practice forgiveness.** Mayo Clinic chaplain, Katherine Piderman, writes that

letting go of grudges and bitterness makes way for compassion, kindness, and peace and leads to "healthier relationships, greater spiritual and psychological well-being, less stress and hostility, lower blood pressure, fewer symptoms of depression, anxiety and chronic pain, and lower risk of alcohol and substance abuse." It is physically impossible to be in a relaxed state and experience anxiety. The states are mutually exclusive. Likewise, resentment and peace cannot be experienced simultaneously. Those who are unforgiving pay the price by carrying that negativity to every relationship and experience. When you are ready to heal yourself and make way for compassion and understanding, mindfully consider your feelings and consciously choose to forgive. You then release the control the offending person has had on your life. Enjoy the freedom.

"Forgiveness is the fragrance that the violet sheds on the heel that has crushed it." Mark Twain

6. **Getting involved. Successful parents consistently encourage participation from their children challenged with autism.** Renowned thinker and science fiction writer, Robert A. Heinlein wrote, "Don't handicap your children by making their lives too easy." It is definitely easier to just stay home, especially if your child struggles with disturbing behaviors. But parents who push through the hard times in public provide novel and stimulating educational opportunities for their children with autism. In Norman Doidge's book, *The Brain That Changes Itself*, we are reminded that scientists know physical exercise prolongs extant neurons while exposure to new experiences, environments, and challenging thinking promotes

neurogeneration of glial cells. With experience and practice, these neuronal pathways set tracks and quicken with speed as a sled going down a snowy hill. **Parents who assist their children with autism in gaining exposure to novel environments and thoughts promote brain growth and development.**

Some parents rarely take their children out as they may make people uncomfortable or disturb others. This is not beneficial to the child or society in the long run. **More than most people, our citizens with autism need practice connecting; yet, ironically, we often give them less opportunity than neurotypical children who also need time and experience to learn how to behave.**

Consider giving society the opportunity and practice to become better citizens of the world, too. When Barb and I are out, I diffuse critical looks by loving her and tending to her more. This technique maybe hard for parents who see their children's behavior as a reflection of themselves.... Let that go. Let the individual's value as a person stand alone. You be the person with them enjoying their company and helping them navigate the situation as best as possible. **We teach people how to treat us.** For example, Barb and I were on a long flight and she inadvertently rocked and kept pushing the seat of the man in front of her. His perturbed grumblings grew. Finally, with an exasperated sigh and verbal notice to his traveling companion, he said, "That's enough!" before laboriously turning his sizeable, no longer young body fully around to give her what for. We knew what was coming. That split second bought us just enough time for Barb to hand me her handkerchief (which she uses to stifle her tourettes) so he would catch me tenderly wiping the drool off her chin. He deflated. The man saw that she was doing the best she can with what she has. Then—so did he.

7. **Generosity. Happy parents are generous**. They write books. They start nonprofits. They serve on boards. They fund grants and organizations. They speak, cook, teach, play golf, network—whatever talents and resources they have—they share. Successful parents are part of the solution. The Dalai Lama states, "Helping others does not mean we do this at our own expense. Wise people want happiness. How to do this? By cultivating compassion, by cultivating altruism. When they care for others, they themselves are the first to benefit—they are the first to get maximum happiness. That's real wisdom."

8. **Meaning. These parents know what has meaning**. Barbara Rentenbach (aka Smother—Barb's Mom) is one of the lionhearted parents I have come to know and respect and is a huge inspiration for this chapter. A couple of years ago, I reported that Barb was slacking off writing and other goal-oriented tasks and seemed primarily concerned with socializing. Barbara said, "Well, is she happy?" I sheepishly admitted, "Yes—very." Our conversation was over; this client had what she wanted.

"Happiness is the meaning and the purpose of life, the whole aim and end of human existence." Aristotle

9. **Perspective—Healthy parents choose accountability over victimhood.** As Victor Frankl writes in *Man's Search for Meaning*, "In the concentration camp, every circumstance conspires to make the prisoner lose his hold. All the familiar goals in life are snatched away. What alone remains is 'the last of human freedoms'—the ability to

173

'choose one's attitude in a given set of circumstances."
Parents can do this.

10. **Relationships. Successful parents have good relationships.** *We are what we connect to.* Physicist Aaron O'Connell writes, "Quantum mechanics says that everything is all interconnected. Well, that's not quite right, it's actually more than that. It's deeper. It's that those connections to all things around you, LITERALLY define who you are."

Your relationship with yourself is the cornerstone. Parents remind us we must stay well for our children. True. Therefore, your energy reserves must be replenished. Taking time for yourself does that while simultaneously teaching your children, "This is how you take care of yourself." Exercise, do things with friends, have intimate time with your spouse, laugh, sleep, eat well, have hobbies, and enjoy life. Live the balanced life for yourself and as a model for your children.

The next relationship priority is that with your partner. The greatest gift you can give yourself, your spouse, and your children is to have a fulfilling marriage. David Code, family therapist and author of *To Raise Happy Kids, Put Your Marriage First* writes, "Families centered on children create anxious, exhausted parents and demanding, entitled children." **Like pity, child-centered families (even child with autism-centered families) are not empowering. Teaching children they are the center of the universe–especially those with special needs, harms development.** Putting your partner first not only benefits the union, it also benefits the children by modeling healthy adult relationships and providing a more stable, harmonious, and loving home environment. Children with autism are often hypersensitive to the moods and emotions of others. As parents, the less tension and negative emotions we can off-load onto our children the better. Take care of your partners. Together, you will strengthen each other. Make this relationship primary and be a united front. Share intimacy, the bed, private discussions, laughter, tears, and support. It takes work and consistent commitment—what outstanding lessons for parents to live and teach.

Successful parents also have rich, plentiful relationships with children, friends, and community. They are not isolated. They seek and maintain networks of support and positive interactions.

To date, connection is the best treatment for Autism. Live it and teach living it to your children.

*Charles and Rachel Prislovsky (Lois' parents) full of optimism and
forgiveness as they let go of trying to raise me motorcycle
free and we simply enjoy our relationship and
appreciate what has meaning.*

Chapter 19

Demons in the Rear View Mirror

Last chapter, I included a quote from George W. Bush. He fascinates me. We have much in common besides being not such great speakers and taking full advantage of career opportunities our families subsidized. We share strong minded and accomplished parents. We are our parent's namesakes. Our fathers were military pilots and our powerful, silver-haired lioness mothers are named Barbara. Likewise, we gratefully experience a close relationship with our parents and write about feeling their unconditional love. Furthermore, Bush admits his alcoholism was based in selfishness. I am not alcoholic but share selfishness as a vice if not a demon. Dorothy Parker may have combined George and my proclivities as Marion Meade explains Parker's frequent hangover hallucinations in her 1989 biography, "It was inevitable that sometimes she awoke suffering from what she termed the 'rams' and felt scared to turn around abruptly for fear of seeing 'a Little Mean Man about eighteen inches tall, wearing a yellow slicker and roller skates'."

Before I transition to my little mean bevy, allow me to remind the reader of my profound loneliness and lack of purpose that fueled my selfishness to addiction.

Do friends exist? For over three decades of my life, they did not. I'll discuss the semantics of realness and existence momentarily. For now, I casually mention how I spent my last four days. I love Monday mornings, as they are a fresh start, yet filled with rich recall of weekends, which I design.

Last Thursday evening, my Jewish Christ mystic (JCM) buddy, Elizabeth, celebrated her birthday with a few close friends at a local margarita watering hole famous for heavenly spinach caso. We went during happy hour, of course, as Elizabeth is a Jewish background believer, which means she believes Jesus is divine and never pays retail. She invited me several days prior and we e-mailed back and forth with fun details, making the dinner crescendo all that more exquisite. The next night, I went out and listened to live music with another couple of friends, Jessica and Rachael (who, incidentally, is also Jewish, but only enough to come away with great hair and lots of education). They e-mailed me a week ago, wanting to "get together soon to buy me a drink." God, I love e-mail and free drinks. And on Saturday...my handsome professor friend and neighbor, Jeff (no Judaism or hair), invited me over to enjoy a party for his art students. I got to know him through Ty and SS and now, we all go on group vacations.

Most writers would never dream of mentioning who they hung out with that weekend or how they met their core friends as it seems too mundane. And it is for most people. But, I am not most people.

To me, weekends like this far surpass any oversized check presented by Ed McMann, which truly would be something to write home about since he died in 2009.

Many of us with Autism ache for what seems a lifetime for real, nonpaid friends.

Can you believe it? I hit the Powerball friend lottery. It is not that I feel undeserving of true friends...it's that I never imagined it would happen for me. Navigating social nuances and connecting warmly and with humor is hard when one can't speak and has faulty body control.

It started with one friend and then gradually, connections spread with practice. I am getting the hang of this.

I do not take friends for granted. Take care you don't either.

I am whole now—well, almost. I do long for romantic connection—more on that later. But before friends, I was so forlorn and bedeviled that I allowed my anger and resentment to wickedly manifest by way of conjured ideas.

Ideas are memes. They are real. Just as words are real. Words are memes or ideas that are expressed. This concept was made clear to me by Dan Dennett, a philosopher who lectures on the dangers of memes. He teaches that concepts are literally alive. I concur. This tale is about dangerous ideas that came to life.

Throughout human history, people die for ideas—politics, religion, discovery, vanity, prejudice and etc.—the list of examples is as endless as the concepts that literally take life.

It is not my intention to spread deadly ideas like my adventuring ancestors who wiped out indigenous civilizations with tiny "harmless" viruses to which they were immune. My aim is neither to annihilate demons, but rather to inoculate with knowledge so toxic ideas need not infect and harm.

In *The First Paul: Reclaiming the Radical Visionary Behind the Church's Conservative Icon* by Marcus J. Borg and John Dominic Crossan, they report a strong scholarly consensus that the "pastoral letters" of 1 and 2 Timothy and Titus accredited to Paul were not actually written by him but in his name several decades after his death. If I am blessed to have my writings extant posthumously (and that is my ambition), then "Demons in the rear view mirror" may temp speculation that this chapter was not actually written by me who changed my name from Barbara Ruth to Barb after my road to Damascus experience at age nineteen, when I became able to communicate with facilitated communication. The critics would be on to something. "Demons in the rear view mirror" was not written by Barb alone as Barbara Ruth made a cameo to make this chapter almost two decades after her death in 1992. The channeling was not easy as all, including Barbara Ruth, are happy she is gone. This world was no place for Barbara Ruth. This world has a place for Barb because I am pecking it out one key at a time.

As Paul surely regretted his Saul sins of youth, so do I concerning Barbara Ruth indiscretions. Each birthed many godless ideas into action. With Barbara Ruth, it started innocently enough. Who am I kidding—no, it did not. Barbara Ruth's fury with God about her abandonment and ridiculously wired body consumed her. Forgive me Father for I have sinned....

My name is Barbara Ruth. I am twelve years old. Dear Dad (DD) smiles at me often with tired eyes and assures in his steady CEO voice, "It is all right, Barbara Ruth, I've got you." Oh, how I wish he did. But no one has me. I am free floating yet far from free.

A couple of years ago, I had the good sense to tether myself to the prison yard so as not to lose my way back to the protection of my cell. DD only sees me during yard time and he never notices my ankle chain. Being directionless and shackled with just enough slack to hang myself is scary as I am at the whim of all—rarely knowing what comes next. I chained myself because although my self-imposed solitary confinement cell is bleak, it keeps me safe from the general population.

The general population is overwhelming. I can't communicate with them. I am affiliated with no particular gang. I try to learn their signs and pick up meaning in their slang and glares. But it is slow going. I am vulnerable.

I ache to communicate and be connected to a pack. I am alone.

Mostly, I dwell in my mind cell. Damp, cold, gray stone surroundings are my best defense against barrages of barks, wickedly sharp colors, painful textures, and yanks of confusion. I know I am alone, but being lonely in the presence of others is humiliating and sears my nerves with madness—so I leave. Mom describes my bedroom as "cute, cute, cute." Two large windows adorned with saltwater taffy colored tapestries drench and yellow all the heat with southern rays. Fluffy, well-vacuumed throw rugs pad the hard wood and tile in the attached bathroom. Powder blue porcelain corrals water for many uses. This is not where I do my time—it is too exposed. I secretly go deeper and can escape to my cell fortress from any "real world" portal, "cute, cute, cute" or otherwise. I leave my Barbara Ruth shell to fool the guards and buy time. When I take it with me, the hunt is on too quickly.

I beg no pardon.

There is routine, but it leads nowhere and always circles around. My time in the yard is bittersweet. Time passes best when I busy myself collecting warmth. I harvest it from sunshine direct hits, close bodies, breath-heated bed comforters, popping fires, yeasty bread, summer backseat car ovens, slippery bathwater, and steaming pasta. But loud yard dogs are always a problem. Boarder collie teachers herd me this way and that, nipping at my heels. Sometimes, I go their way. Sometimes, knowing I have nothing to lose, I fang back. DD is a large alpha yellow lab who nuzzles me to direct and oftentimes just to enjoy my smell. Mom is my almost constant yard companion and guards me from others and myself. She is slight and her fur, thick and warm but often bristled, as this German Sheppard is all business. She bites. I stay close to her. With her, I am safe but not free.

Things changed one Sunday afternoon following a particularly pissy bout with God whom I know exists, but won't permit me access. I was sad. I was mad. These words come to me now on loan from Barb so I may confess. But Barbara Ruth never had words, that is why I was put to death. Sensations were all I had until....

I was lying face down on my moldy cot back in my familiar mental cell. I sensed another. I am always alone here. What the Hell? Indeed. A boy—of sorts—was in my cell, watching me. With his eyes still fixed on my heaving back, he bent and retrieved his baseball. We did not speak. He was there for me. We both knew that. He tossed the ball at my head. It hurt. "Get up. Let's do something" he chirped to my mind in perfect clarity. Then it happened. Our thoughts swirled and merged and I began to know him. His name was Odious. He is sixteen and is playful, strong, and aggressively obsessed with having fun. Odious is not human, although with me he looks pretty close. His bellicose eyes give him away as there is no white part—just shiny black. What the Hell? I'll play. We spent the next couple of hours pounding glass and anything else that would break or dent with that boomerang baseball. After shattering the last guard tower light, he paused and let me know that he was bored and invited a girl over. Miscreant appeared. She is a little older than me and wickedly pretty. Miscreant is a manipulative liar and mean-spirited in every way. I want to be her. Her cruelness pervaded me instantly. I felt the weight of her evil, but carried it well because I was motivated to not be alone. We were thick as thieves for longer than Barb cares me to mention. Barb also forbade me to recount even a glimpse of our shenanigans with Miscreant. As I aged simmering in hormonal broth, another creature came calling—or did I call him? It was the latter.

Nefarious is most complicated. Nef is a sexual hybrid and deviant. Nef is mid-thirties and has been around the block. Unspeakable perversions have soiled Nef so that it leaves a greasy charcoal-like residue on all that it touches. Nef's thoughts on God had my head spinning. Nef carps that all nature is a duality: light/dark, good/evil, matter/antimatter—so what's the point of all this churchy judgmental kerfuffle? Nef teaches me like an experienced school marm except with hairy muscular arms and a neon blue boah. He presents that logically, God is not one entity, but two, just like everything else as it then quickly rattled off a biblical quote that seemed right, Genesis 1:26 "And God said, Let us make man in our own image after our likeness." I may not have bought all the Catholic Church was selling me the last twelve years, but something other than monotheism never occurred to me.

My cell was a busy place those days. I liked the action and loved not being alone. One day, the obfuscating cell clouds gave way and I sensed fresh warmth. I am a connoisseur of warmth and this was nectar. As my pupils squeezed to pin pricks, I noticed another. Lucent is maybe thirty, beautiful with pronounced features, warm and bright. The others scamper when he is near. He moves with grace and illuminates the cell like a tasteful Tiffany lamp as he glides about. Lucent is not human either, but he is more—not less. He smiles softly, but won't speak to me. Did I call this guy? I don't think so. The whole room knows he was always there. This rock was built on him.

I'll stop Barbara Ruth there. We shall keep this tale simple as the devil is in the details. In *The Screwtape Letters*, C.S. Lewis advises "There are two equal and opposite errors into which our race can fall about the devils. One is to disbelieve in their existence. The other is to believe, and to feel an excessive and unhealthy interest in them" (pg. IX). I agree and found the trouble with demons is whether or not you believe they are just in your imagination is irrelevant. They are tough to shake. Demons seek to take. Source seeks to give. Lewis' aforementioned book may be intended allegorically, but I think he may have learned these truths firsthand as I did. Lewis' fictional demon character, Uncle Screwtape, writes to junior devil Wormwood, "We want cattle who can finally become food; He wants servants who can finally become sons. We want to suck in, He wants to give out. We are empty and would be filled; He is full and flows over. Our war aim is a world in which Our Father Below has drawn all other beings into himself: the Enemy wants a world full of beings united to Him but still distinct" (pg. 39).

My road to Damascus experience sent Barbara Ruth packing, but not the creatures.

Words bought me day passes and human companionship so I spent way less time in prison than did Barbara Ruth. But she left me keys and I would be lying if I claimed never to rub elbows with these cell mates again. Although I am sure lying during confession is as common as juice stains in minivans, it seems pointless to me, so I will continue with my unbecoming truths.

Nobody wants to be alone. I am guilty of going too far to end my isolation on more than one occasion.

The entire greeting card industry makes it evident that humans celebrate connection. Think about it. All cards and their floral, stuffed animals, and candy cohorts are all about reaching out and connecting with others. Somewhere amidst the Belated Birthday, Get Well Soon, and Pet Sympathy sections, Autism got overlooked. Where are our anniversary cards? "Another year and you still can't wipe your own autistic ass." Happy Kwanzaa: "What a blessing that being black is the least of your worries." Thinking of you: "Glad I am not you." Wedding: "Sorry, you will probably never be in love, get married, or laid."

That last one has really stuck in my craw. I long for passionate intimacy. Friends are great. But, like most humans, my body and mind throb for more.

About a year ago, I allowed myself to believe that mature romance and sex at last could happen. I fell for a guy who worked with me. Let's call him Mr. Hope. His job was to help me work out physically and study more history and philosophy. I was able to type with him immediately. He was open and not ashamed to be seen with me. I was very attracted. Mr. Hope is Brad Pitt kinda fine– undisputedly hot. The reason I thought I had a chance was he was so very kind and spiritual. I thought maybe this guy can see past my faulty phenotype and want the real me, warts and all. We seemed to be connecting well and were ninety pages into writing a book together. So, communication was not a barrier. He knew I was smart and funny and seemed to like me. I wanted to be with him in every way. I made an intricate plan to seal the deal (aka mistake numbers 1—10).

Mr. Hope is part of the "God Squad"—a term SS and I use to refer to a loose network of young, well educated Christians who sacrifice real money careers to follow their idealist dreams and serve our downtown community. My guy is such a committed "God Squad" activist that he is "saving himself" for marriage and often sublimates that libido energy to professional mountain climbing excursions where he donates all the proceeds to victims of child sex slavery. I allowed myself to imagine that we overripe virgins (perhaps the only pair this age found outside of captivity) could come together and make each other whole for a lifetime.

I calculated he loved the knight in shining armor role and knew Mr. Hope was clearly proud of his close relationship with God so I paired the two and designed a "save Barb and run off into the sunset" scenario. I had not considered the demons that kept me company during bleak times in many years, but now was the perfect time to revisit them to bait the hottie Christian calvary. Mr. Hope was indeed interested in my dark disclosures, which vamped up our winnowing of theological and personal spirituality discussions for months. He showered lil ol me with lots of serious and loving attention, because clearly, I needed help—strapping God Squad kinda saving. We shared secrets. So far—so good.

My coquettish plan was to play hard to get and claim to be hesitant to end my relationship with the creatures because I did not want to be alone. Mr. Hope was supposed to assure that he would be there for me and I would never be alone again. Then we were to work through some kind of healing ("exorcism" is too strong a word, as I never went so far as to claim possession—just collusion). My godly hero was to save me and then sweep me off my beautiful (on the inside) feet. He would be revered for his courageous faith and would gain saint-like recognition for our beauty and the beast union. Senator John Edwards, before his fall from grace, would have nothing on the good press my man would enjoy.

The problem was—Mr. Hope's cooperation. While trying in earnest to be on an otherworldly level of spiritually and compassion, he still had two red-blooded feet in this world and beats to a different drummer—a pretty, tidy, normal girl beat.

He quit.

Benumb my heart.

Before he could officially run for the hills in good conscience, Mr. Hope had me share our stygian secrets with SS to pass on the torch of rehabilitation. She was not amused. SS owns the practice where all this "absurdity" was being discussed and written about for several months. She wanted no part of this fire and brimstone blather in her shop or anywhere else. I was surprised, but she wasn't angry or disgusted with me…it was more like she was protective. I began to feel bad for my would-be hero. SS was not impressed with his role. When he offered no solutions, our meeting was over.

After Mr. Hope left, SS was quiet and extra gentle with me. She pulled her thoughts and emotions together and quickly let go of her resentment about having this mess dumped on her. We both know SS and Barb are a lifelong duo and this was just another chapter in a very long book.

Before we could resume working on other things, SS insisted we meet with my parents to lay all my evil cards on the table. I am grown and we don't involve my makers in all therapeutic comings and goings, but SS thought this one merited everyone being on the same page. I had no objections. That meeting with SS, Smother, DD, and myself turned out to be a godsend. Mom was not judgmental or freaked out at all by my bombshell confession. I could not understand why I was getting a pass on all this. Smother's Virginia Slim-mentholated heart missed no beat as she calmly explained that supernatural stuff does not scare nor interest her because she is not even sure of its existence and quite frankly has other more pressing "real things" to do. Smother chalked it up to me having a crush on a hyper-Christian and a florid imagination. She moved on. She crossed her legs, took a drag, and gave Dad the floor, "Mike?" Surely, my dear Catholic Dad will be worse for the wear. "Your daughter is hanging out with demons" can't be easy news for an upstanding church and community leader. Well, you could have knocked me over with a sparrow's fart. DD's love and council was equally steadfast and unemotional. With quick clarity, he said, "Barb, we all have demons. Want me to describe mine?" And he did! He looked up at the ceiling and began describing some poor devil's, size, shape, outfit, and job description. What an imagination on that one. DD even went on to confess some of his "devil made me do it" sins—

granted, they were vague enough to be said in front of Mom, but I got the message. My parents did not forgive me. They felt no need. They gave me unconditional love. They are my rocks in this world. I stood tall on this foundation and let my board members know I was now ready to leave childish manipulations behind.

There was still the matter of pest control.

SS was relieved at my parent's reaction. I think her Southern Baptist upbringing had visions of me being disowned waltzing cryptically in her God-fearing head. Supportive parents and my resolve to change had her back in her psychologist saddle. Next visit, SS had me get right to work on taking control of my life and ridding myself of that which does not serve me well. Her plan was to have me gradually shrink and make the creatures become more cartoonish, becoming not powerful but ridiculous. We accomplished this with cognitive therapy in about two weeks. Every session, SS would take a few minutes to have me describe vividly the progressive demise of each. It was empowering. I often laughed aloud recalling Bill Cosby's line "I brought you into this world, I can take you out." It worked perfectly. I am 100 percent demon free.

Two months later, while reading C. S. Lewis's *Screwtape Letters*, I ran across these stand alone quotes just thrown in before the Preface: "The best way to drive out the devil, if he will not yield to texts of Scripture, is to jeer and flout him, for he cannot bear scorn." Luther

"The devil...the prowde spirite...cannot endure to be mocked." Thomas More

Don't you just love finding out later that something you bought and were really pleased with had the "Good Housekeeping Seal of Approval"? It is affirming. That's the way I felt about my cognitive behavior extermination plan.

Before I give SS too much credit, let me share that I think she had advice in making such a wise and effective plan. These days, I, too, am permitted access to light help. Thanks God.

G.W. Bush and I are proud to have put our demons behind us. Mr. Hope passed on me but hope has not passed me by.

It is really all about exclusion. The good news it that exclusion is in the eye of the beholder.

Richard Rohr in *Falling Upward* writes, "Beauty or ugliness really is first of all in the eye of the beholder. Good people will mirror goodness in us, which is why we love them so much. Not-so-mature people will mirror their own unlived and confused life onto us, which is why they confuse and confound us so much, and why they are hard to love. At any rate, it is only those who respond to the real you, good or bad, that help you in the long run. Much of the work of midlife is learning to tell the difference between people who are still dealing with their issues through you and those who are really dealing with you as your really are."

This understanding is why I did not allow my middle-aged self to become angry, or too hurt recently when my own brother took his doubting Thomas role a step further and formally asked not to communicate with me anymore via supported typing (ST) in e-mail or in person. He does not believe in ST. Which crudely translates—he does not believe that it is me doing the typing and thinking. Tom thinks I am mentally deficient. I will work hard everyday to show him differently. Meanwhile, I can live with that—because I always have. Almost 100 percent of my teachers thought that way and treated me accordingly—as a lesser being. It only took one teacher who taught from her heart to my heart to change my reality and course. Andrea Reynolds assumed my value and competence. Then so did I. Others followed suit. Today, I choose to no longer allow myself to be excluded from humanity by such perceptions I do not share. So, I continue to practice my independent typing and do not fret about my invitation being lost in the mail. There are other parties I would rather attend.

(Note to teachers—and we are all teachers: It just takes one. Be that for someone.)

Concerning romantic love, my hope is also evolving. The more practice I am allowed connecting with normals, the more I feel the truth that the joy of life is a dish best shared. Soups on.

I considered the personals, but fear a WSM (woman seeking man) ad like: "Independently wealthy, autistic mute on Depo-Provera seeks long term intimacy" may open the door too wide.

Demons, drunkards, horny autistics—oh, my. Before you ban this book, please consider Wally Wojtowicz, Jr. a man about my age who struggles with autism and almost complete ALS paralysis. He wrote in Sally Young's book, *Real People, Regular Lives: Autism, Communication, and Quality of Life*, "Today, I think ALS is how God is rewarding me for my past prayers for deliverance from autism. I look on this episode in my life as perhaps the closest that I will be to becoming a normal human being. I reiterate what I have told other people: My life now with ALS is what I always wanted to be with the exception of being paralyzed. I can now eat with other people without grabbing their food or drink. I don't run away from people upon meeting them. I can be a part of a group without leaving to be by myself. I now can look into someone's face to let them know that I am happy to be in their company. I can now look into another's eyes and pierce their soul with my gaze. I can now be happy and content to feel another person's cheek press mine, or to feel a soft kiss on my forehead, or to feel someone's hand holding mine. All of these little things that most people don't think about I can now do and take pleasure in. Yes, I miss the freedom of movement, but I now enjoy these people who I see. I am now as close to being 'normal as I will be. God has answered my prayers."

Mine, too. I just have to be patient. One doesn't want to look a gift source in the mouth.

Practical Implications:

1. We are all teachers.

2. Live and Love what you teach.

3. Teach to the Heart from the Heart like God is Watching. As I peck out this thought, a newly acquired word (I am a collector) scampered across my mental vestibule, "felicity": 1. Intense happiness, 2. The ability to find appropriate expression for one's thoughts. Ah hah! Felicity is what teachers need to consider when planning differentiated instruction. Remember who you are and what you are here to do. Help your students do that and free felicity.

4. In *Surprised by Joy*, C.S. Lewis conjectured, "Is the future like a line you cannot see or like a line not yet drawn?" I implore you resolved teachers to embrace the latter and get out your colored chalk. It is time to make the future bright.

Demon free Barb calls a family meeting to order. This one is a biggie so I flew in my trusted German, Elke, who can be counted on to take meticulous notes and embolden me with logic and onus as I literally peck out my case for independence letter by letter. The decision went my way along with a significantly increased workload. Beautiful Eleanor Roosevelt said, "Freedom makes a huge requirement of every human being. With freedom comes responsibility. For the person who is unwilling to grow up, the person who does not want to carry his own weight, this is a frightening prospect." I am no longer afraid. Grown, B

Chapter 20
Treat Me—Not My Autism

Tim Sanders makes a case in his fresh book, *Love Is the Killer App: How to Win Business and Influence Friends*, that looking out for number one is not the way to get ahead. Rather, Sanders encourages us to be "love cats" that share knowledge, networks (web of relationships), and compassion (reaching out with genuine warmth). Indeed, we found that being generous with these intangibles helps many individuals with Autism and their families find hope, purpose, connection, and healing.

We do not tout the cure for Autism as to date relief and progress involves perseverance, connection, and commitment. We simply want to share our practice policies that have helped us serve efficiently.

Psychologists and other practitioners are encouraged to adapt: 1. transparency; 2. accountability; 3. mental freshness; 4. humility; and 5. collaborative equality with families and individuals with ASD.

Transparency—as a parent of a son with autism says, "Quit blocking the light."

Webster's defines *transparent* as 2. a. Being free from pretense or deceit: frank, 2. b. Easily detected or seen through: obvious, 2. c. Readily understood, and 3. d. Characterized by visibility or accessibility of information, especially concerning business practices. We concur.

After each session, our practitioners e-mail a summary of what was accomplished that day to the parents and child, if appropriate. All professionals who work with that client are copied on these daily session notes. Our particular company is designed to be "one stop shopping" so we offer a variety of complimenting services. Over the course of long-term treatment, a client may work with a psychologist for the initial assessment, a therapist, treatment specialists, personal trainer, equine specialist, tutors, yoga teacher, and medication management professionals (Footnotes 1 and 2). Parents and clients often choose to forward daily session notes to teachers, guidance counselors, principals, school psychologists, family practitioners, and other support professionals.

We suggest making session notes very detailed, containing specific activities designed for that individual to develop targeted skill sets. We recommend using professional but not overly technical jargon. Therapeutic reasoning should be included, as well as periodic reiteration of treatment goals and progression updates. The intent is to provide clear accounts that may be replicated. What works reliably in session can then be translated to success at home and school with similar exercises. The client then gains momentum. Thinking is linking.

Guaranteed quick response time is also a policy, which promotes transparency and mutual respect. We require practitioners to respond to a client's office contact within twenty-four hours. Accessibility and open lines of communication cost nothing but prove to increase client satisfaction and the bottom line.

By-products of transparency:

1. Smooth Transitions—Clients may relocate or simply choose services elsewhere. Oblige them with useful documentation. The goal is not to monopolize expertise but to add to the client's well-being and overall standard of ASD care. Wherever the client goes, new teachers and practitioners may build on this information.

2. Accountability—If you do a poor job, many people are going to know about it—immediately. If you do an outstanding job...likewise.

3. Competition—Heed the advice of countless business leaders and management books and hire exclusively people who are smarter than you. The next part happens quite naturally as highly competent, driven people inevitably bring their A-game, especially before an audience of intelligentsia colleagues. Partnerships with department heads and program directors at local universities are an excellent way to consistently recruit top candidates in every field. Such collaborations are win—win—win—win. The university is able to offer its outstanding graduate students invaluable practical experience at pay that typically far exceeds university assistantships. A clear win for deserving Ph.D. candidates and the university that is always challenged to bring in top talent. Your clients benefit from young, highly-motivated practitioners just before they become doctors and cost significantly more per session. Your practice enjoys a continuous feed of well-trained practitioners with those who exceed expectations often becoming loyal, long-term partners. Catering the dissertation defense meeting for grad students who work with your organization is another promising idea. It costs relatively little to provide fresh pastries and drinks and is another win-win-win-win. The committee and audience, often a persnickety lot, get delicious snacks, making them sweeter and more generous about passing the doc-wanna-be. Your stressed out scholar feels supported on one of the most important days of their lives (i.e. they will remember this). And with a tasteful best wishes note on your company's letterhead in front of the free food, your group gets direct marketing to colleagues—all helping to spread

the word in academia that your shop is a great place to work.

4. Courting school collaborations—Private treatment is expensive and educational therapy (the primary treatment for autism to date) is not covered by insurance (Footnote #3).

   Copious treatment notes make it easy for teachers to get ideas for helping that student in their class without being "told what to do by some outside expert." When teachers replicate successful techniques at school, our clients benefit from more therapeutic practice at no extra cost. And the teachers look like rock stars. Everybody wins.

5. Referrals—Seasoned professionals may be concerned about the extra, uncompensated time involved in such extensive daily documentation. It is significant. But we find the expense to be worth it in terms of quality control and outcomes. And the bottom line is bolstered as those family practitioners, pediatricians, and other support people with whom the family may choose to share the information...often make new referrals based on their direct confidence.

6. Value—It is not uncommon for people go to mental health professionals and leave without a clear understanding of progress and only a vague grasp of..."Is it working?" Daily multidisciplinary reports make patterns evident. Progress is measured and what is measured is managed. Clients can easily account for how their time and money are spent. They become very informed consumers—empowering.

7. Freedom—Parents may be as involved as they wish. Raising a child with autism is a marathon, not a sprint. Some choose to respond to every e-mail with strategic

praise and diplomatic suggestions. Others simply keep a file for their records. Most choose to multiply their child's treatment practice exposure by doing similar exercises at home. This freedom works well with families as time and energy ebbs and flows in the marathon.

8. Flexibility—What you see is what you get. Families thus have the flexibility to adjust the services at any time to maximize what is working and prune what is not.

9. Egalitarian Communication—parents and providers exchange feedback and ideas freely. Thus, multidiscipline consultations are informed, frequent, and part of the package.

Mental Freshness

Long hours of sustained effort can lead to reduced intensity and burn out. In a perfect world, one wants practitioners to be enthusiastic and inspired to serve with scholarship and compassion every session. This is hard to do, for example, as special educators teaching eight hours a day five days a week. We recommend each practitioner work with a particular client no more than two hours per day. The goal is to have the client look forward to the practitioner and visa versa. We recommend scheduling multiple practitioners for those clients who receive extended care with one practice or institution. Two-hour maximum blocks allow the well-prepared practitioner to be fresh and fully present with each client.

Humility

Socrates teaches that we Geeks (or was it Greeks? No matter) may accomplish more by acknowledging we know less: "The ancient oracle said that I was the wisest of all the Greeks. It is because I alone, of all the Greeks, know that I know nothing."

Tim Elmore, author of *Generation iY*, reminds us that mature people are humble and that "Humility is not thinking less of yourself, but thinking of yourself less." To assist others in decreasing self-involved thought patterns and increasing social connections, we practitioners need to do this. Our clients will mirror us as sure as they mirror our nonverbal communications and moods.

Thinking is Linking.

By-Products of Humility:

1. Humor—Humility and humor often go hand in hand. Einstein wrote before his theory was confirmed, "If relativity is proved right, the Germans will call me a German, the Swiss will call me a Swiss citizen, and the French will call me a great scientist. If relativity is proved wrong, the French will call me a Swiss, the Swiss will call me a German, and the Germans will call me a Jew."

   Taking one's self too seriously impairs approachability. As Einstein attests, sometimes we are right—sometimes not. An accepting and playful tone encourages others to take the risk and effort to connect with us by reducing the fear of "not getting it right."

   Recently, MN, a nine-year-old boy with social anxiety, dyslexia, and ADHD asked, "What was the stupidest thing you have ever done?" Never wanting to miss a teaching/connecting opportunity, my wheels spun as I sifted through my mental repertoire of stupid things. A bit surprised about the bulk of that category, I mentally moved on to an age and clinically appropriate category themed, "seemed like a good idea at the time." I shared that when I was about his age, my best pals, Steve and Brian, and I were setting booby traps in our fort. My innovative contribution was to balance a fireplace log atop the door so when an intruder dared to open it– Wham! Log drop on the head (decades before the movie *Home Alone*, I might add). As one with intact frontal lobes may imagine, little Lois soon became distracted with other play tasks and forgot all about the log, so—Wham! Log drop on head. I came to quickly and we resumed play. Later, in the heat of stick gun army maneuvers around the Walker's house, Steve said, "Hey Weezie (We all had nicknames some, more reasonable than others.), didn't you have on a white shirt?" Indeed. Nothing bleeds like the noggin. My shirt was crimson. Mom, a stoic RN who knew how to stretch a dollar, soaked the shirt and mended my scalp. My cautionary tale took maybe a minute and fifteen seconds of his session. In that time, MN practiced being physically still and attentive; related we are all works in progress; observed that it is possible to lighten up about mistakes; learned nothing bleeds like the head; and maybe just maybe put together that it is wise to pay extra attention especially when something seems like a good idea at the time.

Use humor often and encourage the client to do so with myriad positive reinforcements (verbal and non).

Humor is all about connecting. **Connecting is the goal**. Practice Humor! And if you are not a funny person—use that—be funny about that. Dear Dr. Jessica Lester is by all accounts a saint. Our clients adore her and she spends almost every waking hour serving with her heart and outstanding mind...but wow...she can't tell a joke or colorful story to save her soul (Not to worry, one of the benefits of sainthood is that kinda thing is covered.) Dr. Lester knows humor can be a social communication lubricant so she does not abandon the trade. She smiles broadly and literally informs her audience when she is being funny. As in: "What did the zero say to the eight?

Nice belt." "That was a joke." Clients relate to her honesty, genuineness, and literal presentations in a big way. They get her. And she gets them. Connection!

Another good use of humility is to engage with clients where they excel. I worked with OP, a fifteen year-old male with autism and our goal was to help him generate initiative. He had limited verbal production, but was unbelievably good at "Dance, Dance, Revolution." One session, I met him on his turf at the mall arcade where a behemoth Dance, Dance, Revolution machine awaited its master. OP put in his tokens which was all that was needed for the Greatest Show on Earth. For the next twenty-five minutes, that kid moved with otherworldly speed, grace, and intuition. The machine started going crazy with extra graphics, lights, sirens, and talking back—yelling a variety of sassy phrases like, "What are you, an alien?" OP was in the zone of perfect effortless initiation. Finally, having had his fill, the master stepped off the battle-fatigued machine. My turn.

Believe me, I was trying hard and am a decent athlete, but holy cow…I could not keep up! The machine taunted, "What are you, a white Baptist?" I laughed at myself for the duration. OP began to smile and lighten up, too. The adoring crowd that spontaneously convened to admire the superstar with gasps of reverent disbelief….were now much less reverent and laughed aloud at the middle-aged dancing mediocrity.

In half a session, OP and I practiced turn taking and reversed roles. We practitioners are always asking these clients to do what is hard for them and comes easy for us (communication and schoolwork). We are wise to model the behaviors we wish them to develop. Demonstrate perseverance with grace, work ethic, and good humor. As

Mahatma Gandhi said, "You must be the change you wish to see in the world."

This type of respect and interest often leads to sharing. OP and I shared a coke after my schooling. I was purposefully as silent as possible, but OP knew he had my full attention. He stared at his drink, but I wasn't losing him. **I focused where he did.** Then, I got it and asked, "Are you looking at that condensation?" OP raised his head with a burgeoning grin. He went on to share details about the light spectrum he was enjoying in the droplets on his straw. Look for what they are trying to say rather than what they should say. Let clients know they affect the world. In these moments of respectful attention, OP was confident and able to initiate a meaningful two-way conversation.

2. Time and respect—Be on time. Do not overbook and never double book. To avoid costly no shows and tardiness, reminder phone calls plus e-mails to clients twenty-four hours prior to their appointments are recommended. Coach Pat Summit once told me that she tries never to have anybody wait on her because it is a respect thing. Respect others' time and they will respect yours. Being late also adds unnecessary anxiety for many of our ASD clients.

3. Interchangeable offices—In order to keep overhead down and maximize space, practices may consider practical rooms for multiple purposes. Even offices used by full-time practitioners may be humbly offered for use afterhours or on days off. Donating such intangibles to the community is also encouraged. Consider offering your facilities free of charge to research groups and other community organizations to share goodwill. If your practice consistently has more space than needed, why not sublease an office or two to a nonprofit organization. Partnering,

especially with a nonprofit with overlapping clientele, may prove prudent in terms of increasing your visibility, networks, and income.

4. Inclusion—Create an environment that embraces diversity. **Work hard to let your practitioners and clients know that human excellence comes in all packages so they are invited to be themselves.**

5. Learn from mistakes—In *Living Buddha, Living Christ*, Thich Nhat Hanh explains the Buddhist term *vipasyana* (looking deeply) as observing something or someone with so much concentration that the distinction between observer and observed disappears. When we are able to let go of barriers between ourselves and others, understanding is possible. **Once isolation is gone, fear is diminished, and growth is imminent.**

Before learning the aforementioned, I am embarrassed to admit that a few months after going into private practice, I returned a call from a mother concerned about her son. I called her on my cell, while headed across town to pick up Elijah. This is her beloved child's well being we were discussing and I was giving her neither my full attention nor time. As I reached my destination, I heard myself assure, "I know this child." No, I did not. How arrogant! Needless to say, we did not get the opportunity to work with that family. I would like to apologize, but the best I can do is change. Strive to be infinitely better listeners, more compassionate, and generous with time.

When mistakes happen, respond quickly. Listen. Patiently hear opinions on what could have been done differently to better serve. Ask with genuine intent to follow through, "How can we make this right?" Take blame (I was going to write, "Take responsibility," but politicians have bastardized that phrase to mean... "It was not my fault, some subordinate did it, but I am the boss so I will delegate a solution.") Apologize with sincerity. Make it right. Move on. And for heaven's sake, don't brag about making it right. In her book, *Mindset: The New Psychology of Success—How We Can Learn to Fulfill Our Potential*, Carol S. Dweck confirms how a "growth mindset" can change the meaning of failure, not by eliminating the distress, but by taking control of the painful experience so that it does not define you but rather is processed as a problem to be faced and learned from for betterment. **When we take advantage of the opportunity to change and better ourselves, it takes the hurt out of the pain.**

Furthermore, Dweck writes "People with the growth mindset know that it takes time for potential to flower," as she accounts researching Paul Cezanne's early paintings and finding they were pretty bad. It took time for Cezanne to become Cezanne.

When mistakes don't happen and beautifully commendatory feedback rolls in...don't take credit. Praise all others involved. Uplift and empower all who contributed positively, reinforcing quality service at every level. And if that feels too altruistic or soft, one can always relish in Nelson Mandela's conviction that the praise we give others is a reflection of how we perceive ourselves.

6. Local—Considerable research supports that hiring local suppliers and service providers improves community goodwill, name recognition, profit, and longevity as employed people buy goods and services in your area. Instead of hiring a national company for cleaning or tech support, hire local talent. Information Technology departments at nearby universities are excellent places to start shopping for skilled individuals who provide more

personal services at rates often lower than bloated big businesses.

Additional Practices We Find Inexpensive and the Right Thing to Do:

1. Wireless—Provide wireless Internet in lobbies. Waiting parents, caregivers, and siblings will appreciate the option to work or play on their portable devices. It also shows you respect their valuable time and comfort. If your practice has wireless, it is as simple as providing the access code on a courtesy/convenience plaque in the waiting area(s).
2. Fragrances—Ask your staff and practitioners to refrain from perfumes and colognes. Such odors may beset our clients with ASD with unnecessary and unwanted stimulation.
3. **Go green**—Susan Casey writes in *Fortune Magazine* that Patagonia founder, Yvon Chouinard, etched the following quotation from Sierra Club's David Brower on the company's front door, "There is no business to be done on a dead planet." Demonstrate your company's commitment to problem solving with recycling, electronic documents, conservation, environmentally friendly lighting, and a growing number of other options. **Accept the gift of being part of the solution**.
4. House calls—Consider making house calls to minimize your company's footprint while providing a huge convenience to clients, especially those with many young children or severe disabilities. Bill for travel time at the same rate as sessions so your practitioners are fairly compensated. Families appreciate the option and many consider it worth the added expense—increasing

their quality of life and your billable hours. In home sessions, are also mutually beneficial by allowing practitioners dynamic assessment insights to better tailor treatment plans.

5. Cleanliness—At the end of the day, wipe down all surfaces with environmentally friendly disinfectants. This takes little time and money when compared to the health benefits for your clients, families, and work partners.

6. Online opportunities – Consider offering services online as an alternative to home or office visits. Skype™, provides free live face-to-face communication via the computer which is wonderfully efficient in terms of time and travel conservation. With Skype™, clients are no longer limited to support professionals based on proximity. Online services, can match needs based on compatibility, skill set, and choice – regardless of location. More details on this approach may be found on our website: psychoeducationalnetwork.com

As Tim Sanders says in *Changing the World by Business*, "Good is the new Great." Intend to be in business for good.

Treat the person, not their autism.

Footnote 1. Personal trainers and yoga teachers are often part of our full service treatment plans as we seek to serve the whole person. In her book, *Adolescents on The Autism Spectrum,* Chantal Sicile-Kira succinctly states the increased risk for depression for those with autism and offers, "Exercise is a healthier alternative to fighting mild to moderate depression. Research shows that it only takes thirty minutes of aerobic exercise three times a week to reduce depressive symptoms." She explains that exercise raises levels of Phenylethylamine (PEA), which creates a natural antidepressant action in the brain. In addition to improving circulation and thus mental sharpness, exercise provides additional opportunities for socialization and navigating novel environments, which promote neuronal health. Norman Doidge, the author of *The Brain that Changes Itself: Stories of Personal Triumph from the Frontiers of Brain Science* writes, "Nothing speeds brain atrophy more than being immobilized in the same environment: the monotony undermines our dopamine and attentional systems crucial to maintaining brain plasticity."

Footnote 2. Psychotropic medications are part of our practice—the smallest part. Our network prides itself in working with our clients and their families to maximize the salubrious effects of diet, exercise, sleep hygiene, parenting strategies, and a variety of cognitive behavior techniques to minimize medication needs.

Footnote 3. Education is currently the primary treatment for autism. Educational therapy is not covered by insurance. Drugs designed to alleviate many of the symptoms of autism are covered by insurance...but they do not solve the problem. Is this the best we can do as a society?

Being different can generate fresh perspective. (Ty and Lois)

Chapter 21
Conclusion: Fair Share

We are making connecting a habit. Neuropsychologists, Donald Hebb's well known axiom: "neurons that fire together – wire together" fuels our progress. And as Charles Duhigg identifies in *The Power of Habit: Why We Do What We Do in Life and Business*, regular small wins motivate us to change and then those behaviors become automatic. This is how independent typing and this book finally became a reality.

We were asked by a publisher to write a book and made strides to have it complete by November 2011. After almost a full year of work, in October 2011, the publisher withdrew the offer. We were fired. We resolved to better ourselves.

We made a posterboard that reads:

10-25-2011: We are not believed or successful.
So:
Step 1 = Barb types solo (every day fifteen minutes)
Step 2 = Lois studies writing (nine hours every week)
Step 3 = Sell millions of books
10-25-2012 = We are believed and successful

We prop this poster board on the desk each day when we write. We dutifully complete steps 1 and 2. As Duhigg points out, "Once that habit starts unfolding, our gray matter is free to quiet itself or chase other thoughts." Our tasks became automatic and no longer required difficult decision-making. The habit loop of the cue, routine, and reward are working.

The Native American proverb, "Without you, I would not be me," heralds our intent to do more together. So we started a company: Mule and Muse Productions, LLC. We also created a non-profit organization to help re-circulate success. The Greater Living Institute (GLI) is a 501(c)3 designed to work for bright adolescents and adults with disabilities to assist them in maximizing their highest potential. Our plan is to combine our strengths to maximize neoteny and enhanced perception because as Armstrong's beautiful book, *Neurodiverstiy: Discovering the Extraordinary Gifts of Autism, ADHD, Dyslexia,* and *Other Brain Differences* reminds us, "There is no standard brain, just as there is no standard flower or standard cultural or racial group; that in fact, diversity among brains is just as wonderfully enriching as biodiversity and the diversity among cultures and races." We hope remembering "I might be you" may free others to live life on purpose habitually and enjoy a quiet mind and chasing other thoughts.

Practical Implications:

1. For best results - focus your intent and persevere.

2. Mind thy heart to mine thy mind.

3. Richard Branson in his book, *Screw Business As Usual,* coins the term "capitalism 24902" taken from the equatorial circumference of the earth to proclaim a new age of doing business where companies focus on how they can make positive change for communities. Goodness knows – business grows.

Barb Rentenbach and Lois Prislovsky, Ph.D.

Mule and Muse Productions, LLC is open for business for good.

Bonus Chapter
Surprised by Jerry

In *Surprised by Joy*, C.S. Lewis conjectured "Is the future like a line you cannot see or like a line not yet drawn?" I am betting on the latter so I am drawing my line in the sand.

Four days a week for two hours at a time, I work with SS on an array of things and have been doing so for just over ten years now. Progress is consistent but slow and that is not due to lack of effort on either part. I work hard everyday to be my best. My autism does not make it easy and sometimes I am enraged at having to shoulder this way of being. I write so others may know themselves and me and to make both paths more luminous.

Here is an exchange SS and I had just last week, which shows the tedium I dine on regularly:

Session notes: Barb broke her bracelet while I was setting up her independent typing board. Then she sat at the keyboard and broke the pencil and banged the board. I remained calm and asked her to chill on the couch for moment and she did. There she began biting her arm and broke her glasses. Then we had the following dialogue as she gradually deescalated.

b= why do i do that? i liked that bracelet. when i am one with the universe, all is good, but when i feel alone, my eyes fill with pride and ego. i then lose focus and get frustrated. why does it take all my concentration and energy and so much time to type just a few words when 99.9 percent of all humanity does it quickly with barely a thought? why me? i vacillate between happy contentment and frustration and self-pity.

l = what percentage of the time for each?

b = 75 percent content 25 percent frustration and self-pity

l = has that ratio changed over time?

b= big time. it was the opposite when i was a teen.

l = gradual?

b = yea, the last five years steady improvement

l = what about the next five years?

b = good point. i'm shooting for 80/20

l= and in ten years when you are fifty years old?

b = 85/fifteen

l = i see a pattern

b = patterns were my first love. 90/10 at age 55; 95/5 at 60; then i will slow my ascent until i fully awake around 83. you will die at 88. i think i may let go around then when I am 83. depends on my mood.

l = do you wish to talk more about this or would you like to do your daily independent typing now that i see you are happily content again?

b = let's save this for the book, it might help some bloke off a ledge, but yes, i am ready for my independent typing practice.

(Barb bit again a few times, but I gave her some physical space and she worked through it and typed really well. By the end of this session, Barb was all smiles and happy sounds.)

End of Session Note Excerpt

As I ponder how to share my daily struggles, I recall a quote from Richard Daily's *Meditations*: "Wisdom is not the gathering of more facts and information, as if that would eventually coalesce into truth. Wisdom is precisely a different way of seeing and knowing the ten thousand things in a new way."

Wisdom is the freedom to be truly present in what is right in front of you. Children do this masterfully. Presence is wisdom! People who are fully present see justly.

The trick is to be mindful even in aroused states of frustration and fury. At the risk of sounding like a prize terrier, SS has helped train me to regulate my thoughts and actions this way. I peer down from my mental tree house at my unsteady body and behaviors. This perspective is advantageous to self-awareness and facilitates my rickety ladder descent through bitter fogs until I can plant my warty toes in the cool grass.

Nietzsche wrote, "There are no facts, only interpretations."

Perspective is the skeleton key of life.

Take, for example, an article one of my egghead friends forwarded me, written by a regular looking thirty-something named Jay, a self-proclaimed asexual. These folk have no interest in sex. Curious. I wonder if Jay considers himself neurotypical. I am told I am not neurotypical. However, I do have an interest in sex—great sexpectations, actually. But I have had no socially acceptable access (Kinda like Catholic clergy, except it's even harder for me to get some without alerting authorities.).

I find it illuminating that Jay shares asexuals are often perceived "like nonpersons." Is humanity that exclusive? What are the normal majority so afraid of losing or watering down when they restrictively classify what does and what does not constitute a whole human being?

Please take a fresh gander at humanness. What do you see? Do you see Jay? Do you see me?

Romantic orientation, jelly toast, fat, autism, race, religion, having sex, or not— none of it marks the essence of who we really are. Your essence is just as valid as mine.

Being in love has afforded me a new perspective and prescription lens on justice.

As I established in part one of this book, words renewed my personhood. But, my pass was stamped second class. I want an upgrade. It's time for a real relationship and all that comes with it.

The prescription to progress is to set specific, measurable goals. My eyes are on the prize and he is tall and handsome. Like anything else, there are steps. This year, I made the following strides: first date, first real Valentines Day Card, first kiss, first "I love you" (not to family), and a steady march toward my first person amendment.

Here is what most see when they look in my direction: softness—physical and mental. "Wait! I just saw her pick an ant-carpeted Chiclet up off the fairgrounds and eat it. Ugh, this poor gal is not all there." Fact is I am all there and out there, too. See me? I see you—all of you, metrosexuals, asexuals, heterosexuals, homosexuals, hypersexuals, retrosexuals, the whole perfect human lot.

Jerry saw me. He was in the audience at a couple of our Knoxville Public Library presentations. One may wonder how a mute gives a lecture; well, it ain't easy, but apparently, I am getting pretty good at it as I reeled in this tall, handsome engineer. Jerry e-mailed me and we started a warm and respectful dialogue. Then, a couple of weeks later after making sure he had polite conversations with both my parents at the next presentation, Jerry asked me out for a stroll. Old school— my favorite.

At thirty-nine years old, dating was all new to me, but so was having a career, making friends, buying my own home, and traveling when and where I wish until a few years ago.

As Steven Wright muses, "Everywhere is walking distance if you have the time." Time to take that step.

SS was beside herself with joy for me. Some folk naturally amplify your happiness to good news. We giddily cogitated a cascade of possible outcomes for a few minutes but not long enough to jinx it. Then, SS got Ty, her family's secretary of defense, on the background check right away. Ty, cyber stalked Jerry and within minutes found out his age, occupation, degrees, address, divorced status, photos, employment history, license plate, and all manner of useful information to provide the police if necessary. Jerry initially invited me for an evening walk downtown after my next presentation, but Cagney and Lacy weren't having it. Ty and Lois convinced me to plan a daytime double date first so I could ride with them and avoid milk carton fame if things went sour.

My first date was at 11 am at Ijams Nature Center. Never wanting to exclude, SS brought Ty, Elijah, a neighbor girl pal of Elijah's, and that damn stray beagle they adopted a week prior. It was a bit much.

Jerry held my welcoming hand confidently as we toured the gardens. Sensing no foul play, Ty gave us some space and took the obstreperous hound on a long loop hike. SS and the kids also left to climb every tree in the park. Although I was never out of SS's sight, it did occur to me that if Jerry chose murder he could have probably got most of it accomplished before SS descended a sixty-foot elm.

Jerry and I visited the walk through museum and he presented me with a poinsettia (poisonous but no malice intended) and chocolates (confirmed nonpoisonous, as I ate them immediately). Ty returned and unfortunately so did Matthew Beagle. It was almost time to go, when that stupid dog, on the scent of something putrid, fell into the moss pond. This Cinderella's chariot ride home was rank way before midnight. I vowed to travel lighter.

The next couple of dates were beagle free but I instructed my personal attendant to remain within screaming distance (my kinda mute means incapable of productive speech, but this old gal can holler). The third date, I threw caution to the wind and enjoyed my vulnerability with just Jerry. I was falling for this gentle man.

My first kiss was on my swing in my front yard. Jerry is not the kiss and tell type. Clearly, I type and tell.

My first Valentine's Day Card arrived in sail mail. Again, old school.

My first "I love you" happened about a month after V-Day and came at the tail of a beautiful e-mail that I saved for posterity. Wanna see it?

From: Jerry
To: Barb
Sent: Thu, Mar fifteen, 2012 8:46 pm
Subject: An attempt at an encouraging note . . .

This before Smother and Brenda prevent us from ever seeing each other again because they don't want me giving you French fries:

I think you would be an ideal good match for LOTS of guys. If they don't see that, their loss.

Reasons:

Birth Order: Girls with older brothers are supposed to be a good match for guys with younger brothers, and the hard-to-match only-kid. SS *might* know about this, but there is a popular-psychology author named Kevin Lehman who mostly reinforces this that I learned in a college sociology-like class. This alone makes me think you are a 'find'.

Wealth: Lots of guys worry about 'high maintenance' Significant Others, but your health seems to be stable, and your maintenance funded. I gather you don't even want babies.
Talking: Guys complain that girls talk too much. You don't.

You can still write encouraging notes.

Of course, you're not bad-looking either, and don't seem to go for tattoos, strange body piercings, or a black wardrobe.

All of which makes me feel a little like Mario after being kissed by Princess Peach, except for the flu, of course.

—Jerry

my dear mario,
this is the most amazing e-mail i have ever been given. i love your honesty and humor. i did not even laugh when i read it because i am bowled over by my good fortune. i don't know how to respond in a measured way. i feel i must write about our growing relationship right away to share my joy and hope. i pray you are agreeable to that as i can't seem to stop my writing wheels from spinning. i promise to share all drafts with you and honor your privacy in any way you wish. for me, being a writer means literally being an open book, but that does not always umbrella those closest to me. i am going to write now. thank you again for your sublime gifts of encouragement. love, princess b

Okay. I said it first, but it still counts. Guess what he did next? The man offered to give me a key to his place. Now, two can play at the old school game so with an enchanting blush and fluttering lashes, I graciously declined his red-blooded offer. But a girl does like to be asked.

217

Being a late bloomer has distinct advantages. I know what I want. I know what I don't want. I know who I am. And what I don't know no longer gives me anxiety, as it will come in time.

For the most part, the life I have chosen is manifesting at the rate I choose. Patience is a virtue, but for me it is more like a third arm. I was born with it—most are not. I wield it to help me juggle emotions, creativity, goals, personal interactions, and mindfulness. Jerry has a third arm, too, but Aspergers is the only diagnosis most would give him. Third arms are not transparent. All can see them if they wish, but most do not because they are not expecting to see.

I am designed well for my purpose because my third arm and high pain threshold make me well-equipped to harvest justice as it is a slow, painful processes to farm it. SS was assisting my research of positive and negative liberty for background for this piece, when her wife, Ty, came in crying and asked if we could put our work on hold for a few minutes while she got something off her chest. Now, Ty is a formidable woman. She is ex-military, a tri-athlete, fulltime anesthesiologist, resolute friend to me, and a rock in our community. She is no crybaby. As one may imagine, I am a fantastic listener—much better than SS, despite her pro status because she is always strategizing ways to treat and fix. I literally just listen.

Ty tearfully read an article posted on Facebook by one of her business partners presenting "another position to consider" concerning President Obama's statement supporting the right for same-sex couples to marry. The author was dismissive of such families and used crude terms to describe those sex lives. Truth be told, it was titillating, but so much is to the sexually parched. Plus, such acts did not seem exclusive to homosexual couples—but I digress. He went on to accuse Obama of reverse evolution because the President's decision was based in part on how his young daughters perceive families with gay parents as equal. The writer judged divining wisdom from children as ignorant. I understand why Ty's feelings were hurt. Belittling the validity of her family is mean. I expect if Jerry and I marry, our family will also be put in some pile other than the IN Box with full rights under the law.

It boils down to justice. For now, us nontypicals must suffer at the hands of inconsiderate masses because the majority does not grant minority equal rights until all other alternatives are shown unpalatable. So, day after day, I write the bitter truth. Each person who truly hears will find the status quo a little harder to swallow.

Like Ty's kind, my ASD clan needs access to government. I was skipped over for a free and appropriate public education because even though supported typing was allowed for me, an imprimatur was never given permitting my supported typing to count. I moved on and now make my own education count.

This planting season, I am focused on harvesting my legal rights as a sentient adult. As it stands, my parents are my legal guardians. I can't enter in binding contracts without their permission. As love has me considering the contract of marriage, I vote for change.

When my parents are gone, folk expect my brothers will take the reins. Well, not if I pull this horse to a dead stop with my own unsupported hands. To be fair, I love my brothers and they have dutifully let me ride on back of their bikes, 4-wheelers, jet skis, mini bikes and horses, but I am grown now and not always going their way.

My parents know I am preparing the fields and working hard to start tipping the scales of justice to include me. I want to marry. I want to have sex. I have no intention of asking permission. I do not want my brothers to be my keepers. The thought infuriates me. And that's not just my Dutch oven

PTSD talking. One brother thinks I am mentally retarded and living in a sham world of charlatan facilitators. The other is not as black and white, but his saintly wife has a big positive influence on his humanity. Why should I be susceptible to their whims? They don't own me. Or do they? What part of the Old Testament law is our society cherry picking this week concerning my rights?

In James Allen's *As A Man Thinketh*, he writes "Law, not confusion, is the dominating principle of the universe; justice, not injustice, is the soul and substance of life; and righteousness, not corruption, is the molding and moving force in the spiritual government of the world. This being so, we have but to right ourselves to find that the universe is right."

Allen further contends, "Circumstances do not make a person, but reveal him." (We must forgive the sexist language of this 1902 author, but such forgiveness is needed, anyway, for righting ourselves to pick the fruit of justice.)

I embrace my purpose. My autistic circumstances reveal me as no neurotypical, privileged white girl life would. I am just Barb and I am grateful. When I write, it flows from the breeze because it is who I am and what I am here to do. Feelings and ideas funnel through the top of my head and grind down in words. The word drip is slow but rich as I can brew. Best served hot.

The end of the beginning.

Bibliography

Allen, James. *As A Man Thinketh*. NY, NY: Tribeca Books, 1910.

Armstorng, Thomas. *Neurdiversity: Discovering the Extraordinary Gifts of Autism, ADHD, Dyslexia, and Other Brain Difference*. Philadelphia, PA: Da Capo Press, 2011.

Borg, Marcus and Crossan, John Domnic. *The First Paul: Reclaiming the Radical Visionary Behind the Church's Conservative Icon*. NY, NY: Harper Collins, 2009.

Boorstein, Sylvia. *It's Easier Than You Think: The Buddhist Way to Happiness*. NY, NY: HarperCollins Publishers, 1997.

Bradberry, Travis and Greaves, Jean. *Emotional Intelligence 2.0*. San Diego, CA: Talent Smart, 2009.

Branson, Richard, *Screw Business as Usual*. NY, NY: Penguin Group, 2011.

Bush, George, *Decision Points*. NY, NY: Crown Publishing Group, 2010.

Code, David. *To Raise Happy Kids, Put Your Marriage First*. NY, NY: Crossroads Publishing Company, 2009.

Doidge, Norman. *The Brain that Changes Itself*. NY, NY: Penguin Group, 2007.

Duhigg, Charles. *The Power of Habit: Why We Do What We Do in Life and Business*. NY, NY: Random House, 2012.

Dweck, Carol. *Mindset: The New Psychology of Success: How We Can Learn to Fulfill Our Potential.* NY, NY: Ballantine Books, 2006.

Dyer, Wayne. *Change Your Thoughts Change Your Life: Living the Wisdom of theTao.* NY, NY: Hay House, Inc, 2007.

Elmore, Tim. *Generation iY: Our Last Chance to Save Their Future.* Atlanta, GA: Poet Gardener, 2010.

Foer, Joshua. *Moonwalking with Einstein: The Art and Science of Remembering Everything.* NY, NY: Penguin Press, 2011.

Frankl, Victor. *Man's Search for Meaning.* NY, NY: Washington Square Press, 1984.

Gelb, Michael. *Discover Your Genius: How to Think like History's Ten Most Revolutionary Minds.* NY, NY: HarperCollins Publisher Inc., 2002.

Gladwell, Malcolm. *The Tipping Point: How Little Things Can Make a Big Difference.* NY, NY: Hachette Book Group, 2002.

Gladwell, Malcolm. *Blink: The Power of Thinking Without Thinking.* NY, NY: Hachette Book Group, 2005.

Hanh, Thich Nhat. *Living Buddha, Living Christ.* NY, NY: Riverhead Books, 1995.

Hawking, Stephen. *A Briefer History of Time.* NY, NY: Bantam Books, 2005.

Johnston, William. *The Cloud of Unknowing: and the Book of Privy Counseling*. NY, NY: Random House, 1973.

Lamott, Anne. *Traveling Mercies: Some Thoughts on Faith*. NY, NY: Anchor Books, 2001.

Lewis, C. S. *Surprised by Joy: The Shape of My Early Life*. Orlando, FL: C. S. Lewis PTE Limited, 1955.

Lewis, C. S. *The Screwtape Letters*. NY, NY: C.S. Lewis Pte. Ltd, 1942.

Meade, Marion. *Dorthy Parker: What Fresh Hell Is This?* NY, NY: Penguin Group, 1989.

Montgomery, Mary. *Love and Remembrance: The Gift of Animals and Healing from Their Loss*. Minneapolis, MN: Montgomery Press, 2006.

Morgan, Marlo. *Mutant Message Down Under*. NY, NY: HarperCollins Publishers Inc., 1994.

Nadesan, Majia Holmer. *Constructing Autism: Unraveling the "Truth" and Understanding the Social*. NY, NY: Routledge, 2005.

Nicholi, Armand. *The Question of God: C. S. Lewis and Sigmund Freud Debate God, Love, Sex, and the Meaning of Life*. NY, NY: Free Press, 2002.

Palmer, Parker. *To Know as We Are Known: Education as a Spiritual Journey*. NY, NY: Harper One, 1993.

Radin, Dean. *Entangled Minds: Extrasensory Experiences in a Quantum Reality.* NY, NY: Simon and Schuster, Inc. 2006.

Ramachandran, V.S.,& Blakeslee, Sandra. *Phantoms in the Brain: Probing the Mysteries of the Human Mind.* NY, NY: HarperCollins, 1998.

Rohr, Richard. *Falling Upward: A Spirituality for the Two Halves of Life.* San Francisco, CA: Jossey-Bass Books, 2011.

Roth, Evans. *Brains, Religion, and Reality: Integrative Searching for Purpose and Peace.* Bloomington, IN: Authorhouse, 2005.

Sanders, Tim. *Love is the Killer App: How to Win Business and Influence Friends.* NY, NY: Three Rivers Press, 2003.

Sanders, Tim. *Saving the World at Work: What Companies and Individuals Can Do to Go Beyond Making a Profit to Making a Difference.* NY, NY: The Doubleday Publishing Group, 2008.

Seligman, Martin. *Learned Optimism: How to Change your Mind and Life.* NY, NY: Pocket Books, 1990

Sicile——Kira, Chantal. *Adolescents on the Autism Spectrum: A Parent's Guide to the Cognitive, Social, Physical, and Transition Needs of Teenagers with Autism Spectrum Disorders.* NY, NY: Penguin Books Ltd., 2006.

Siegel, Daniel. *Mindsight: The New Science of Personal Transformation.* NY NY: Bantam Books, 2011.

Sinclair, Upton. *Mental Radio: Studies In Consciousness.* Charlottesville, VA: Hampton Roads Publishing Company, Inc. 1930.

Stengel, Richard. *Mandela's Way: Fifteen Lessons on Life, Love, and Courage.* NY, NY: Crown Publishers, 2009.

Young, Sally. *Regular People, Regular Lives: Autism, Communication, and Quality of Life.* USA: Autism National Committee, 2011.

Walker, Alice. *The Color Purple.* Orlando, FL: Hardcourt, Inc. 1982.

Zinn, Jon Kabat. *Full Catastrophe Living: Using the Wisdom of Your Body and Mind to Face Stress, Pain, and Illness.* NY, NY: Bantam Dell, 2005.

Contact Information

Mule and Muse Productions, LLC
2892 Alcoa Hwy
Knoxville, TN 37920
Fax = 865 579-2522
Web Site: muleandmuseproductions.com
Email: info@muleandmuseproductions.com

Direct tax deductable contributions can be made to
The Greater Living Institute (GLI)
at 2892 Alcoa Hwy, Knoxville TN 37920

9 780988 344907